Rush Christopher Hawkins

Report on the fine arts

Rush Christopher Hawkins

Report on the fine arts

ISBN/EAN: 9783741141157

Manufactured in Europe, USA, Canada, Australia, Japa

Cover: Foto ©Thomas Meinert / pixelio.de

Manufactured and distributed by brebook publishing software
(www.brebook.com)

Rush Christopher Hawkins

Report on the fine arts

FIRST GROUP.

WORKS OF ART.

O

(EXTRACT FROM THE OFFICIAL CLASSIFICATION.)

FIRST GROUP.

WORKS OF ART.

CLASS 1. Oil paintings: Paintings on canvas, panels and various grounds.

CLASS 2. Paintings of different kinds, and drawings: Miniatures; paintings in water colors; pastel and drawings of all kinds; paintings on enamel, earthenware, and porcelain; cartoons for stained glass windows and frescoes.

CLASS 3. Sculpture and engravings on medals: Statuary, bas-relief, repoussé work, and chiseled work; medals, cameos, engraved stones; inlaid enamel work.

CLASS 4. Architectural drawings and models: Studies and fragments; representations and plans of buildings; restorations from ruins or documents.

CLASS 5. Engravings and lithographs: Engravings in black; polychromatic engravings; lithograps in black, in chalk, and with brush; chromolithography.

2

C

REPORT ON THE FINE ARTS.

By RUSH C. HAWKINS, Commissioner.

INSTRUCTIONS FROM THE SECRETARY OF STATE.

In a letter of instructions which the writer received from the Secretary of State the following passage occurs:

Your general duty is to make a thorough examination of the articles exhibited in the group of the Exposition to which you are specially assigned, and to report upon the state of such art, science, or industry in the year 1889 as shown in the Exposition. This report will be published by Congress, and is intended for the benefit of the people of the United States. I need not, therefore, impress upon you the necessity of making it thorough and exact, and at the same time of practical benefit to our fellow countrymen.

When the unprecedented magnitude of the display of modern works of art at the Paris International Exhibition of 1889 is taken into consideration, the seriousness of the task imposed becomes bewilderingly apparent. The working portion of the lifetime of the best equipped art writer living, faithfully bestowed, would not be sufficient for the success of such an undertaking.

ADVERSE INFLUENCES.

The value to the people of the United States of a report such as the one required seems to the writer to be open to question. Even if it were prepared by a scholar versed in the arts and equal in capacity to the best living writer upon those subjects, it is doubtful if it would exercise any perceptible influence upon the education of public taste. The crushing power of unprecedented enormous wealth concentrated in the possession of a comparatively small number of our population, and the conceit it engenders in the minds of its possessors, constitutes a sort of intangible Chinese wall, which stands as a barrier against general improvement in matters of taste and artistic adornment. The process of the cultivation of this powerful class to a fair standard of civilization, their conversion from a belief in the meretricious in art to an intelligent appreciation of the lastingly beautiful must at best be of very slow growth.

3

ART IN THE UNITED STATES.

Unfortunately for the artistic reputation of our country, testimony fully sustaining the truth of this statement is far too abundant, and we need to search in but one or two of our fruitful fields for illustration. Our public statues, groups, and other monuments erected to perpetuate the memory of distinguished men, heroic deeds and great events, and purchased (often at enormous unprecedented expense) as works of art, constitute one of the most discouraging chapters in our national history. Of the many hundreds and possibly thousands of such works which exist on our soil, it is quite safe to assert that there are not more than twenty-five which, from an art standpoint, are fairly good. Prominent in this great aggregation of base ornaments, and perhaps the most offensive because of its great size, is the common place pile erected to President Lincoln at Springfield, Illinois. It is so ostentatiously weak in nearly every respect that instead of its being accepted as an object of interest and veneration, it must be regarded as a curious pile devoid of intended significance or artistic expression. Its astonishing groups of statuary, heroic in size, are bronze monstrosities of unprecedented hideousness.

The Gettysburgh battlefield, the future Mecca of the North American Continent, its sacred soil consecrated to a great cause by the blood of thousands of heroic men, is now in reality a field of perpetual horrors which neither wind, storm, nor time will destroy. Let us hope that the sacred associations surrounding these attempts at appropriate commemorative monuments will in the future prevent the motive being mistaken for one of caricature, and that the lofty desire to justly honor noble deeds which was the primary cause of these violations of good taste, may be accepted as a mitigating excuse for their existence.

The capital of our country presents another field of investigation to those in search of the monstrous in art. From the time of the Mills statue of General Jackson and the erection of the cast iron dome of the Capitol, to the present day, the stream of bad statues and worse architecture has continued to flow in upon a historic soil hallowed by the memories of many decades filled with great events.

WASHINGTON AS AN ART CENTER.

We are compelled to regard Washington as one of the art centers of our country for two sufficient reasons. The first is that it contains more statues and public monuments than any other city in the United States; in the second place, it has within its boundaries a greater number of large and important public buildings than any other American city. In addition to its open-air monuments it possesses a chamber of horrors which contains voluntary contributions in the form of statues from the several States composing the Union, such as in any of the countries of Western Europe would make the fortune of a second Madame Tussaud. This certainly is the most curious collection of unartistic and possibly semi-grotesque specimens of marble cutting ever assembled under a single roof.

Most of the products of the brush which are supposed to ornament the Capitol, are fully up to the level of the Government statuary. They were born of a period of our history when debased politics, ignorance as to the value of the beautiful, and want of patriotic pride in the æsthetic reputation of a nation, prevented the legitimate and natural growth of a love for the arts.

WASHINGTON ARCHITECTURE.

The majority of the later examples of architecture paid for by the people's money are, as to art value, quite as low down in the scale as the statues. Since the erection of the Patent Office Building there has been a steady deterioration in intelligence of design and sense of the beautiful. Let us hope, however, that in the new Pension Office the downward extreme has been reached, for it certainly does seem that deeper into the depths of the commonplace or of the barn-building style we can not go. The existence of a cast-iron dome resting upon a stone semi-Greek monumental structure, both having to be painted white every year, the new National Museum of no particular order, but bearing a remarkable resemblance to what a large beer-garden might be. and the new pile west of the White House ought to have satisfied the reasonable desire of any government in search of the truly original. But it seemed that their presence only served to whet the appetite of our public officials for more, and in order to satisfy their longing the Pension Office Building had to be raised. Let us console ourselves with the belief that in the existence of this structure we see the culmination of the decadence of architecture in Washington.

BANK NOTES, COINS, AND STAMPS.

There is no excuse for our not having better bank notes, coins, and stamps, which if artistic in design would prove valuable object lessons for improving public taste, but so insensible are Government officials in charge of certain departments to the value of the beautiful in its application to every day life, that it has never occurred to them to give the people an artistic bank note in the place of the detestable "greenback," a silver or composition coin of beauty, or a postage stamp above the level of the lowest commonplace. There can be no reasonable excuse for this neglect. A change for the better is only a matter of small expense and art knowledge enough to enable a Government agent to select artistic designs.

STATUES AND MONUMENTS GENERALLY CONSIDERED.

New York, Boston, Philadelphia, Brooklyn, others of the larger cities, and possibly nearly all of the lesser ones, have erected to national and local notabilities, regiments, companies, or batteries their full share of public monuments. In this race for open-air statues New York has fairly outrun her sister cities, and of her achievements, as of those of Washington, it may be said that the latest are the worse. The first statue raised in New York of any value as a work of art was the equestrian of Washington, by H. K. Brown. It is remarkable for its dignified repose and its simplicity of design, and as a whole fairly represents the greatest American. The latest statue erected in that city is one intended to represent Garibaldi in his historic fighting costume. It is far worse than any of its predecessors, and so thoroughly does it lack intelligible design that we may safely say that in the descending scale from the Washington statue its place is the lowest. Possibly, however, the large amount of money now being raised for a monument to General Grant may create an opportunity for realizing still worse results.

By the number of its pieces of statuary, Boston, with oft-repeated claims for superior culture, comes next to New York, and shares the sister city's bad eminence in art matters. It is admitted that among her two or three dozen works there is one of real merit. This is likewise an equestrian statue of Washington. The others are up to the usual dead level of American commonplace, and if interesting at all, it is because they call to the mind of the beholder a great event or a notable name, which object could be as well attained by the carving of an inscription upon a slab of marble.* If Boston has failed in her statuary, it must be admitted that she has been more successful than other American cities in her buildings, of which there are a considerable number, public and private, that are worthy of admiration. Such structures as Trinity Church by Richardson, and the Boston Public Library now in course of erection, would do credit to any community, and their existence will atone for a long list of sins against the canons of good taste in other directions.

AMERICAN ARCHITECTURE.

The cities of the West and South show no improvement upon those of the Eastern and Middle States. Their architecture for domestic and business uses is bad enough, but that of their public

---

* A bill is now before the Massachusetts legislature embodying an appeal signed by a large number of citizens of Boston and by one artist, J. Foxcroft Cole. It asks for a commission which shall have power to accept or reject public monuments before they are completed, and settle where they are to stand. The mortuary monument to Colonel Cass, which was foisted on the Public Garden of Boston, has roused the citizens to this act of self-protection.—[February 15, 1890.

buildings is infinitely worse, because of the greater size, and of the fact that they are as a rule incrusted with rude, uncouth ornamentation, and meaningless projections. The average American architect fairly revels in projections, and is seemingly never so happy as when put in possession of a twenty-five by a hundred feet lot and told to go ahead, regardless of expense. In a few months he will have succeeded in producing a front garnished with cornices, a considerable assortment of moldings, miniature pediments, semicolumns with capitals to match, and the whole completed by a massive flight of steps of sufficient dimensions for a large public edifice. Another peculiarity, fully developed from one end of the United States to the other, is the wood and zinc cornice painted and sanded to imitate stone. This device originated in the double motive of vanity and economy—the desire to get a large amount of show at the smallest possible cost. One of the natural sequences of these makeshifts is the mixed front of stone or brick and iron. These materials often come together, and when they do the parts composed of iron are usually regarded as ornamental, and are sometimes painted white so as to shine out in strong contrast with the red brick by which they are surrounded. The so-called "Grand Central depot" in the city of New York is a *brilliant* example of this exclusively American style. It can not be denied, however, that of the many thousands of buildings erected in the United States every year, a very small percentage of fairly good specimens of architecture could be selected. But it is certain that an exhaustive search for simplicity and reposeful elegance in the designs of either public or private edifices would not be attended with any considerable degree of success. Such an examination, however, would prove the one supreme fact in connection with our architecture, viz, that the average American architect upon nearly every occasion expresses his dislike of a plain surface.

OUR NATIONAL NEED OF ART CULTURE.

The preceding brief general statement, partly in the nature of an introduction, has been written for the purpose of bringing to the foreground in this report the great national need of sufficient art culture in our country to enable persons of ordinary intelligence in other matters to select designs for public and private structures which shall not be offensive to a hoped-for coming standard of fairly refined public taste, and shall at the same time form parts of an attractive whole when regarded as items in the composition of a city. What we require is a standard of culture which would compel the erection of artistic buildings and enforce the acceptance of better designs for public monuments. But the question how this is to be brought about is a complicated one, and clearly can not be solved by a report upon conditions rendered apparent by art collections at a universal exhibition. The task of reforming and elevating the taste of a nation of sixty-five millions of inhabitants is not an easy one, and it will never be accomplished by the fine writing of elegant essays or the compilation of circumstantial reports. The reform will, at best, progress slowly, and must in the end come from an inwardly acknowledged necessity, rather than from outward pressure.

(1) The most careless observer of to-day will find many stubborn obstacles standing in the way of any considerable degree of improvement in art education. Among these may be set down, in the first place, the fact that within the last forty years the intercourse between America and Europe has increased a thousand-fold, and that the art perceptions of our people, as expressed by visible manifestations, are not as refined as they were before this means of easy and frequent intercourse existed. Conclusive evidence to sustain this assertion exists in the many thousand of overdecorated, overfurnished, overupholstered, ugly residences of a numerous wealthy class. These manifestations of the way to "overdo" it prevail in every city and considerable village from Maine to California, and it must be acknowledged that the conditions which bring about such results are to be found in the combination of wealth with that semi-barbaric desire for show that is indifferent to sham.

If this statement be true, it proves that our frequent intercourse with the refined nations has not improved our art perceptions, and would seem to indicate that we are beyond the influence of example.

(2) The vanity incident to and born of suddenly acquired wealth is a sort of *ignis fatuus* which leads the new-made man of millions to believe that he is really superior to his fellows, and now constitutes such a powerful element in our social structure that it has become a national misfortune. Those who form the millionaire class have worked themselves to the conviction that the same faculties or series of accidents which, as a rule, had placed unearned millions to their credit, would, if used in other directions, render them masters, without serving the necessary time to make them expert workmen. The perfectly well-defined assumption of superiority and right to leadership which in the United States pervades this acknowledged all-powerful class, is a formidable obstruction in the path which might lead to a high general plane of intellectual development, and it would moreover neutralize to a considerable extent any general movement in the interest of refinement in matters of art.

The statutory restriction upon the importation of works of art has, to a very considerable extent, barred out essential elements which must be a part of any scheme for our higher education in æsthetic matters. It has raised up a class of dishonest tradesmen who, presuming upon the credulity born of ignorance, produce rubbish which is passed off upon those unable to discriminate, and in

most instances takes a place which should be occupied by works of
real value. The same desire for the artistic adornment of one's dwelling that impels the purchase of a sham, would induce the buying
of something really meritorious. In this relation as in others that
could be cited, the operation of the thirty per cent. act has become
especially vicious. It has created and encouraged the production of
bogus pictures, and it indirectly assists a newly fostered set of knaves
to cheat the ignorant. We may search in vain the history of western civilization and of legislative enactments for a parallel of this
provision against the arts. It is the only instance where the law-
making power of a great country has interposed the force of its will
against the free right to acquire those productions of genius which
are the most valued possessions of the refined nations, and its existence in our statute book may be regarded as an extreme illustration
of the emptiness of our pretension to occupy a higher position in the
history of the civilization of the nineteenth century.

In Italy the Government retains the right of controlling all works
of art, ancient and modern, which are in the country, and none can
leave it without an official permit. In other European countries
government competition is frequently encountered when really good
works are offered for sale, and so strong is the love of the artistic
among the European peoples, that those who produce notable works
are esteemed public benefactors. These conditions arise from a belief that a cultivation of the arts refines, and that a love of them
assists to soften, the hardness and aggressiveness incident to the commercial occupations of everyday life.

An important condition to be completely established before we can
hope for any general elevation of ideas relating to the arts in the
United States is, that every person shall have the right to purchase,
free from Government tax, and to bring into the country any
acknowledged work of art not produced by mechanical agencies.
That such works are luxuries for the wealthy, and are purchased for
the personal gratification of the buyer, is no argument against the
unqualified right to acquire and to import. It would certainly be
better if the General Government, the States and municipalities were
to obtain them for public collections; but of course the American
citizen of average intelligence knows that so long as the nation is
ruled by " practical politics" no such desirable end can be expected.
The people have the right, however, to demand of their rulers that
such laws shall be enacted as would in every way encourage the citizen to enrich his collection, since it is from private possessions that
the majority of the existing public galleries in the United States
have been formed. Therefore, the writer is clearly of the opinion
that the repeal of the thirty per cent. act would do more in the direction of fostering and encouraging a national taste for the arts,

than hundreds of reports setting forth the condition of art in foreign countries.

ART IN FRANCE.

Profound admiration and a lively sense of appreciation of official duty compel me to acknowledge the greatness of a refined nation, whose energy and spirit devised the means and method for bringing together within its boundaries the greatest and most comprehensive collection of material for object lessons ever assembled. Whether it be regarded as an unusual opportunity for the amusement of the casual observer, or a great school for the student, the success of the Universal Exhibition of 1889 is one of unparalleled splendor and completeness. If the exhibition has proved one fact more than another, it is that in the world of art the French have reached a higher standard of true excellence in many respects than any of the other nations. While several have retrograded to a level of commonplace, the French have achieved a steady advance, and no year, of late, has passed without showing new evidence of the substantial value of their schools, the industry of their students, and the good effects of intelligent Government supervision, together with discriminating national patronage. This last is bestowed with a free hand, not only to enrich the museums of the larger cities, but also for the purpose of forming good collections in many of the lesser towns. To good instruction and liberal patronage may be ascribed that continuous and lively interest in everything that pertains to the artistic which seems to pervade all ranks of the French people. A good record at the art schools, and a hope of substantial Government recognition, are incentives for hard work, and they induce a constant striving for higher degrees of excellence.

EXTENT OF ART INFLUENCE IN FRANCE.

It must be clearly understood that these references to the state of art in France are not made upon the narrow lines of the professional art critic, who as a rule writes only technically of particular objects. If we would rightly comprehend the full force of all that has been accomplished by the schools, we must accept the entire results of artistic training in their broadest and most minute significance. We must look into and study their relations to the everyday life of the people. Here is an especially fruitful field for observation, for within its boundaries we shall have occasion to examine everything in use for personal comfort and convenience. In domestic architecture we see general uniformity of design, of which the chief characteristic is studied simplicity. The whole consists of a combination of simple lines, flat surfaces, moderate projections, unobtrusive ornamentation, and, when needed for actual use, balconies. The interiors, according to well-established principles, correspond to an acknowledged national formula as to convenience and comfort. They are subdivided with especial reference to economizing space and insuring a liberal amount of light and ventilation, and are, as a rule, appropriately decorated in accordance with the dictates of refined tastes. In the better French houses—those occupied by the upper and well-to-do classes—the stuffs and furniture are always artistic, and they often rank high enough artistically to be regarded as beautiful creations of the imagination. Never in these residences do we find a ceiling overloaded with a combination of crude colors expressing a complexity of kaleidoscopic design, the whole meaning nothing, and showing nothing but a confusing surface of meretricious stencil ornamentation, born of bad taste and unlimited bank account, and a desire for something worse than barbaric display.

REFINEMENT OF DAILY SURROUNDINGS.

Refinement of daily surroundings is the most important among the elements needed for the superior education of the individual. A boy nurtured and brought up under the influence of good forms and harmonious colors would, when he reached the adult period of life, be perfectly certain to select the most artistic productions for his own home. The knowledge which enables him to do this is the result of direct contact, but it comes imperceptibly, without effort or special teaching. These surroundings make men and women more considerate, kind, and reserved in their intercourse with each other, and help to give refinement to the transactions of everyday life. Prize-fighters, wife-beaters, and tobacco-chewers are not results which flow from the source that irrigates the arts. No doubt the *salon* has furnished its share of characters whose names are to be found in the world's record of crime, but their misdeeds have scarcely been on the level of the brutal murderer's, or those of the sneaking cut-purse.

HOW TO HELP THE WORKING CLASS.

The practical solution of the slum question in the large cities is almost as far off now as it was fifty years ago. The success attending the efforts to improve the condition of the world's unfortunates who fester in fetid holes has not kept pace with the increase of their number. Church organization and governmental methods to raise the morals and ameliorate the physical condition of this burdensome class of human beings have not shown the best results attainable. But now a new light is breaking through the clouds; the comparative uselessness of the old theories and methods has become apparent, and there are tangible indications of a fresh departure in a practical direction, which, if developed on a large scale, may prove to be of

inestimable value to the most unfortunate of the toiling classes of
society. The liberal bequest, now intelligently directed, of the late
George Peabody, for the erection of workingmen's homes in London,
not only set the fashion in England of giving money with a similar
end in view, but led the rich and benevolently disposed to think
about the best method to be employed in order to secure the substantial improvement of the classes intended to be benefited.

MODEL HOMES FOR WORKING PEOPLE.

The erection of the first group of houses from the Peabody fund,
and their immediate occupation, showed beyond all dispute that a
move in the right direction had been made. These buildings were
well ventilated and lighted; the rooms were of fair size, arranged in
convenient groups, and let at moderate rents. As fast as ready for
occupation they were eagerly sought after by people of the working
class, whose mental and physical condition has been greatly improved by the change. Several of the most recently erected of these
workingmen's homes, built by London philanthropists now living,
exhibit a considerable advance in the matter of internal arrangement
upon those first constructed out of the Peabody fund. One occupies
an irregular quadrangle of goodly size, with a court in the center,
where are to be seen, a fountain, flower-bed, turf, and group of shrubs.
The building fronts upon four streets. Every room and passage is
well ventilated and lighted; there are bathrooms and closets with
water in abundance on each floor. broad flights of stairs with graceful turnings at each stage. The carpenters, masons, and painters'
work is appropriately artistic, and sufficiently ornamental to comply
with the reasonable requirements of refined taste. The whole is of
a most cheerful and inviting aspect, and to those who have been used
to rearing families in rooms 7 feet by 9, these homes must seem an
earthly paradise. The building described is not far from one of the
lowest quarters of London, and is largely occupied by former inhabitants of a well-known slum. Their conversion to decent habits,
and reclamation from the lowest depths of depravity, was almost
immediate. The first indication of improvement usually showed
itself in a growing appreciation of cleanliness. and then, in regular
order, came less drunkenness, less wife and child beating, and less
foulness of speech. With these signs of improvement was observed
a gradual development of a love for the beautiful. Money which
a month before would have been spent for drink, now went for a pot
of flowers, sometimes an engraving or photograph, a piece of china,
or a bit of glass. The artistic and comfortable surroundings which
the poor pack-carriers for the more fortunate classes of humanity
found in their new houses, turned out to be the true harbinger of
peace and rest, and the most potent expression of good will from
man to man.

Here we have the proof that it is possible in less than one genera-
tion to raise from the lowest state of ignorance, wickedness, and
despair, a large class of human beings whose depravity seemed to be
beyond the reach of human aid. Are we not compelled to admit
that in this particular field, so fraught with good results, it was the
application of the artistic to comfort which constituted one of the
chief factors in the transition ?

If this proposition be granted, why not urge upon our successful
stock-waterers, unprecedented land-grabbers, and the magnates of
trusts the importance of an extension of this application of the arts
to the useful, in the interests of the poor, and also as an expiation
for their numerous offenses against the interests of States and the
rights of citizens ? In no better way could their ill-gotten gains be
disbursed, and in no other manner could they so appropriately make
some reparation for their gigantic crimes. If in the future it should
appear that the reading of this report had caused one of these
offenders to offer substantial evidence of his repentance, then, in the
words of the Secretary of State, it would have proved to be of "practical benefit to our fellow-countrymen."

RURAL HOUSE-BUILDING IN AMERICA.

There is also another sphere in which a little knowledge of the
art may be usefully applied; this is a broad field, worthy of the
utmost cultivation. In the rural districts of the United States, from
our northeastern boundary to the southern end of California, we are
afflicted with complications of ugly rusticity in dwellings, without
parallel in other countries, which may be designated as the national
makeshift wooden shanty architecture, so cheap to build, so expensive to keep in repair, so cold in winter and so hot in summer.
First and foremost amongst these, standing out in its offensive relief
against land, water, sky, and forest, is the white painted, peaked-
roofed, enlarged dry-goods box with green blinds, which a want of
imagination in our early New England ancestors caused to be
handed down to posterity as a dwelling house. No doubt when this
curiosity in rural house-building was invented, its inventor congratulated himself upon the fact that he had found a way out of
the log-hut period. But what a mistake! While the one is an insult
to all the beauties of nature by which it is surrounded, the other, on
the contrary, erected on the green sward and buried picturesquely
among the foliage of the forest trees, blends into and completes the
beauty of the general picture, like a part of nature necessary to the
scene. Often the owners of these habitations, not taking into consideration that the offense of such objects existing is bad enough,
add to it by placing them as near the street or roadside as possible,
where there is neither shrub nor tree to neutralize the chill their
presence inspires. This location is often selected with the motive of

saving land where it is comparatively worthless; add to such a house a flanking fence of long rough boards, nailed to posts at right angles and whitewashed, and the picture is complete.

Another, and if possible, even worse monstrosity than the house in white, is the architectural effort of the great man of the village who has made his mark in the circles of finance. He often affects the elaborate, but does so with the scroll saw and the paint pot. With these he will produce a rare jumble of cupolas, false and real chimneys, seeming gables supported by iron rods, variations upon Dutch roofs, balconies everywhere, piazzas on all sides, heavy projecting cornices, etc.; each part painted a different color, and the whole when completed suggesting a serious attempt to combine for domestic use all known mathematical forms. But the owner is usually satisfied, for he knows he has got the worth of his money, and that in his own woodpile all colors and forms are represented.

With us there is much important work for art to do outside of its influence in shaping the appearance of material things. Its mission is not only to add grace of form and correct color to things in daily use, but also to infuse, if possible. just a little sentiment into the never-ending roar of the mills which grind for mammon only. Perhaps a new departure in the interest of the arts would soften the hard, metallic, almighty-dollar music to which the whole nation is now so proudly and boastfully marching.

UNPROFITABLE TRAVELING.

Our people seem to regard art as an abstraction instead of a living and useful quantity, and the majority of them are satisfied with a rapid foot-race through European museums of painting and statuary, which they count as pleasingly curious. They congratulate themselves upon having "done" the Louvre and the Vatican, and at the end of the "grand tour" are sincerely glad that the business of sight-seeing is over. Their contract with themselves as to time and territory to be covered being completed, they return home to resume their usual occupations, to build as ugly houses as ever, and fill them with as inartistic furniture as those in the possession of their untraveled neighbors. Their foreign travel has been of no value to them in the way of education, for now, no more than formerly, do they stop to reflect that a handsome chair, a pitcher of good form, or a carpet showing artistic composition of colors and design, need not be more expensive than the badly designed rubbish presented for their approval by the ignorant manufacturer, whose machines merely respond to the creations of his untutored mind.

METHODS OF IMPARTING KNOWLEDGE.

The painter of a fine picture and the creator of a great statue are entitled to very high places in the records of civilization; but the interests of their works in this materialistic period of the world's history is very limited. They exercise no perceptible influence in forming the sentiment or elevating the morals of communities or nations. Professional writers, art critics, curators of museums, dealers in art, and the very wealthy purchasers of artistic works, are about the only classes affected. The art work, the need of which is chiefly felt in our century, must come from active agents; a fine picture hanging upon a wall, or a noble statue standing upon a pedestal, are important elements in a general scheme, but an unlimited number of collections, composed of the best works, would never reform the taste of a great nation.

INFLUENCE OF THE SOUTH KENSINGTON MUSEUM.

In the South Kensington Museum—with its means and adjuncts for teaching—we have an illustration of what can be done by an active vital force. In its short existence it has accomplished more for the general diffusion of art knowledge and love of the beautiful among English people than all the inactive art collections of Great Britain put together. The reason of this is neither remote nor obscure; it exists in the fact that it is a vital force, while the others are a passive quantity only. The South Kensington Museum injects its influence into the everyday life of the people; the others invite the gaze of the lovers of the beautiful and curious, but are like preachers whose sermons are delivered with folded arms and closed eyes.

That great school, founded by the late Prince Albert, one of the most thoroughly enlightened men of our time, became at once a potent influence in the cause of art among the people of the British Isles. It has proved of inestimable value to them, and its influence is now felt in the remote corners of Her Majesty's dominions.

THE BEST WAY OF SPENDING THE SURPLUS.

The United States need at least three such collections and schools; one for the East, a second for the Mississippi Valley, and a third for the Pacific slope. And there can be no better way of "getting rid of the surplus" than by expenditures judiciously and intelligently made for the establishment of such schools, to be placed under Government control. Our people are now forming what might be appropriately called in social geology the palace strata. What better business can our National or State Governments engage in than that of educating not only our fast-growing class for the palace strata, but likewise all classes of our people, up to a certain standard of knowledge concerning art values, as necessities which ought to find expression in our everyday surroundings?

The artistic should be the rule, the inartistic the exception.

THE UNIVERSAL EXPOSITION OF 1889.

The Universal Exhibition of 1889 will pass into the history of the nineteenth century as one of its greatest achievements. It was conceived and carried out in a spirit of catholicity far beyond that of either of its predecessors, and became such a success as to entitle it to a notable position in the history of civilization. In such an enterprise no combination of individuals, however powerful or wealthy, could have accomplished anything like the measure of its completeness: only a united and enthusiastic people, proud of their nationality and traditions, working together for the accomplishment of a great object could have achieved such a brilliant triumph.

. It is difficult to decide which department stands first, in the estimation of those capable of judging, or which was most complete. In almost every sphere where human energy has been applied the best that has been done was represented, and under those temporary roofs the student in search of knowledge could have found nearly all that has been accomplished in every field of human endeavor. The sciences, arts, and industries were fraternized; and no path trodden by the genius and industry of man was neglected.

Never before in such variety and quantity have the productions of the arts and manufactures been brought together; never before has it been so difficult to decide where the industrial arts leave off and where the fine arts commence, so imperceptible are the dividing lines, if they exist at all. The field of the industrial arts has of late so broadened, and it now comprehends so much that there is practically but a thin partition between them and the fine arts proper as heretofore recognized. In many of the industrial sections were displayed works of various kinds which in design and execution showed an art value far superior to that of some paintings and statues in the *Palais des Beaux Arts*.

This assertion is particularly applicable to tapestries, silk stuffs, carpets, made-up dresses, laces, combinations in furniture, wood carving, metal work, designs in gold and silver smith's work, ceramics, and glass. The men who composed the designs for some of these beautiful things for daily use were, in many instances, artists of no mean pretensions, thoroughly educated, possessing great creative power, and worthy of places in public estimation quite equal to those occupied by gentlemen who spoil canvas with paint, and those of another kind who, without the art instinct or the education of a school, build bad statues to order at so much per ton.

TENDENCIES OF MODERN ART.

It can not, however, be admitted that the best in an artistic sense now produced by industrial processes is better, more original, or as good as in the past. During the Renaissance in Italy, and at a later period in France, the application of the beautiful to the useful was carried to a degree of perfection not since attained. What may be said of the present is this, that there is less imagination among painters, sculptors and designers, and more general knowledge of *technique* than there was three hundred years ago. The effort now seems to be to send art down to its original starting-point. Painters are doing the work of the photographer, but with brush and palette instead of with a camera. Nine-tenths of them paint only what they see, and never what they feel, for they feel nothing; never what they imagine, for they imagine nothing. The manufacture of a salable commodity seems to satisfy their craving for the artistic; and, judging from their works, we are forced to the belief that their inspiration, if they have any, comes from matter rather than from the ideal. They transfer to canvas in a mechanical way just what they see. External objects are always to hand. The artist tries to copy, but does not compose or construct pictorially a work of art. His *technique*, which the schools and ateliers teach him, he regards as a very useful stock of tools. His teaching answers the same purpose as does the regular outfit of a carpenter when he leaves his apprenticeship and commences business on his own account. It is a lamentable fact that a very large majority of the artists of the present day start out like the carpenter, to make a business, and apparently care very little for art.

INFLUENCE OF ART DEALERS.

The natural result flowing from this indifference to the poetic and imaginative in art, is a gradual sinking down to a low level of realism, void of design, interest, or intellectuality. To this state of things no set of men have more persistently directed their pernicious influence than the dealers in art. No other fraternity during the last quarter of a century have more successfully sounded the depths of the pockets of the new-made millionaire. than they. They have filled the art world with false gods which fools in abundance have fallen before, and created and encouraged manias which have taken deep root and fructified in the rich soil of ignorance and mammon.

Facts illustrating the truth of all this could be cited by the hundred, but a very few examples will suffice. Twenty-five years ago the portrait of a trunk of a tree in the forest of Fontainebleau, painted by Diaz, brought in the United States about twenty-five dollars, sometimes as much as fifty. Soon after his death the dealers succeeded in putting such performances up to about a thousand dollars, and they have remained near that price ever since. It has been stated that at the time of Corot's death, a certain Paris picture dealer had on hand a hundred and twenty-five of his works, and other dealers in that city were also well stocked with them. The body of the dead artist had hardly time to cool when the dealers' "boom" started, and within a very short period they succeeded in putting up the price at least twenty-fold, and from out their dark corners they supplied good, bad, and indifferent Corot's, to an almost unlimited extent. Even now, a canvas with the name of this artist upon it, no matter how weak, false, or indifferent in execution it may be, will bring an enormous price, entirely out of proportion to its real value. But the great marvel of the nineteenth century in the way of creating fictitious values is best illustrated by reference to the sales of works by Millet. Good, bad, and indifferent alike bring prices far beyond those previously paid for the best modern masterpieces, and of the old masters only the "Blenheim Raphael" has sold for more than the price said to have been paid for the "Angelus." It seems incredible that the works of this artist, the very large majority of which are devoid of grace, interest, imagination, or beauty of any sort, and have often been executed without much regard to the correct drawing of the human figure, should command the enormous prices they do whenever they are offered for sale. The "Angelus" is an exceptional work, for there is in that a charm of sentiment, and an expression of the reverential, seldom found upon canvas. The way in which the hour is expressed, and the attitude of the figures, are in perfect harmony with an admirable idea.

Couture was once asked his opinion on Millet's works, and the following was his answer: "To-day we see a canvas upon which is uncouthly painted a rough peasant standing before a log of wood ; three months later we see upon another canvas, the same peasant with the same log of wood upon his shoulder : three months after, upon a third canvas, there appears the same log, but this time upon a fire, and our friend, the peasant, as badly painted as in number one, is standing in front of it and looking at it burning, and so ends, in three chapters, Millet's great story of the peasant and the log of wood." Nothing could more thoroughly express an absence of imagination than this graphic description by Couture, so perfectly in accordance with fact. To the writer of this report, Millet's work seems in an inartistic and imperfect manner to express only the grossest, most unpicturesque, and most uninteresting realism. His subjects, as a rule, were unworthy of a great master ; his human types nearly express idiots or monsters, who could not have existed out of asylums, and if the portrayal of them exercises any influence at all upon humanity, it is quite certain that it neither elevates nor refines. The boors of Teniers the younger, Steen, Brouer, Adrian Van Ostade, and Hals, are infinitely more interesting than those of Millet, and to-day the works of these great artists give us a better insight into the habits, manners, styles of dress, ways of living, and amusements of the common people of their period than all the written histories of the Low Countries ever printed. While the men and women of the Dutch and Flemish artists are often found in interesting groups, dancing, singing, and otherwise having what might be called a "good time," those of Millet are generally engaged in such operations as carrying sick calves, hog-sticking, an idiotic monster leaning upon a hoe, etc., in which the majority of mankind do not take the least interest.

THE SALE OF THE "ANGELUS."

Apropos of the subject, and while the ink with which the foregoing paragraphs were written was still drying, something characteristic occurred in Paris. The Secrétan sale, which had been worked up to white-heat point by two shrewd firms of Paris picture-dealers, aided by paid experts, auctioneers, newspapers, and art critics generally, as no other sale had ever been before, was about to take place. The penny-a-liners asserted in their most authoritative style that the whole world was on the tiptoe of expectation and feverish anxiety as to the coming fate of the "Angelus." Monarchs were supposed to have passed weeks of dinnerless days and sleepless nights, tormented with anxiety; senates and parliaments had adjourned pending the great event, and whole business sections of great cities had abandoned their usual occupations, until the momentous question should be settled; while, according to the newspapers, this painful suspense was imperiling the peace of Europe, there came a chilling trumpet blast from England which in tones portentous told to the startled European art worshipers the discouraging news of the arrival of the agents of the Corcoran Art Gallery of Washington upon the shores of Britain. They, like some awful giants of fabled story, were coming to carry off the coveted treasure which all the nations of the earth were determined to own. Then was heard the thrilling story of their late landing at Queenstown, their catching of the Irish mail, their hiring at Chester of a special train for $400, which carried them to London at the rate of 64 miles an hour, and then of their further timely advance upon Paris, much to the consternation of the monarchs and the rest of European mankind. By a singular decree of fate the "great sale" commences immediately upon their arrival ; but the 500,000 francs which they bid, did not (fortunately) obtain the immortal work. A self constituted-agent of the French Government succeeded in capturing the prize for the sum (on paper) of 553,000 francs, which his Government very promptly and properly refused to pay. The gigantic farce ended by the "inestimable treasure" going into the hands of a firm of New York art dealers for the rumored sum of 580,650 francs.

The authorities of the Corcoran Gallery are to be congratulated upon the failure of their agents, who had shown their willingness to pay $100,000, in making the most thoroughly foolish and unwarrantable art purchase ever known. The enormous amount of money which they were willing to so misspend could have purchased fifty

of the finest examples of works by the best living masters, which
were then for sale and to be found in the *Palais des Beaux Arts* at
the Exhibition. These works if purchased and placed upon the
walls of the Corcoran Gallery, would at once have made that collection the great art feature of our country.*

THE OBJECT OF WHAT HAS GONE BEFORE.

The preceding portion of this paper has not been written in strict
accordance with the terms of the letter of instructions. The writer,
however, has followed his instructions to the letter in this; that in
trying to point out what to do and what to avoid, he has had the
benefit of the people of the United States constantly in his mind.
But the stage has now been reached for considering and reporting
upon the state of art in the year 1889 "as shown at the Exhibition."
An exact compliance with this part of the instructions would compel the writer to devote to it the rest of his life; consequently an
exhaustive, specific, technical report upon particular exhibits, will
not be attempted. What follows is a general statement, somewhat
historical, in relation to teaching, institutions, and remarks upon
the present condition and plans of the fine arts, as illustrated by
the most important objects shown at the Exhibition.

THE TECHNICAL STRENGTH OF THE FRENCH SCHOOL.

At the threshold of this investigation stands the fourteen hundred
and eighty oil paintings which represent the last eleven years' work
of the great body of living French artists. Although the works of
some notable painters are not included, the collection may be said to
cover the field. It is chiefly remarkable for its technique, which
certainly in no assemblage of modern art has been surpassed, if
equaled. Here is clearly told the triumphant story of the school,
its masters, and the high standard of work demanded from their
disciples. Nearly every canvas indicates a fair amount of severe
training in mastering the elements; and while only a comparatively
small number of works have reached general excellence, a high
standard of the merely mechanical part of the art of painting is
plainly apparent. In painting, as in every other branch of human

---

* Not many years ago there lived in an Eastern city a man who posed for a great
artist, and the community in which he lived accepted him at his own valuation.
One day he died and soon after his studio effects came to the hands of the auctioneer.
A gentleman of one of the interior cities of the State of New York, an affected "art
lover," who desired to possess one of the "gems" that had fallen from the great
man's easel, attended the sale and carried back to his home a piece of rough paper
smudged over with charcoal. Up to this day neither the owner nor his art-loving
acquaintances have been able to decide which side up this seventy-five-dollar "gem"
should be hung. This anecdote illustrates the average common sense involved in
the usual "art craze," and is here cited as a warning. In countries where the
English language is not spoken art manias, as occupations, do not succeed.

endeavor, the accomplished student or the expert mechanic may turn out a coldly correct piece of work, but it is only the genius or man of exceptional talent who, besides knowing the mechanics of his calling, is inspired by a wealth of imagination which enables him to astonish the world with a great masterpiece. This universal rule is as applicable as ever it was in the past to the French artists of to-day, and if it were not for their splendidly equipped and exacting school they would possibly produce no better technical work than their struggling brothers who live in countries where there are no schools, but where each individual worker strives to be a school unto himself.

ARTISTIC INSTINCT OF THE LATIN RACES.

Therefore it would be surpassingly strange if, under the favorable circumstances which surround the French art student from the outset of his career, he did not produce better results than are achieved in other countries. But it is not to the school and masters alone that he is indebted for his exceptional success. He, first of all, has for art purposes, the advantage of being of the leading Latin race, which is a great help to him, gained by the mere accident of birth. That there is in the human race such an intangible quality as the art instinct there can be no reasonable doubt; and that it has been more marked and strongly developed among the Latin races than among the northern people, is also indisputable. If the history of art proves one thing more than another, it is the value of this instinct in the development of painting, sculpture, and architecture among the southern races. To the influence of the Greeks, and, in later times, the great era of the Italian Renaissance, is the northern part of the civilized world indebted for much that is good in its art achievement. But in no country has that double influence taken such deep root and retained such vigorous life as in France; in no other has it produced such far-reaching and beneficial results. In that country it has kept alive a natural love for the artistic, which even in these materialistic days of steam and iron adorns every phase of national life.

THE INFLUENCE OF GREEK IDEAS.

Jacques Louis David, born in 1750, was called by his countrymen the head, and also restorer of the French school. It might more appropriately be said of him that he introduced into French art a correct knowledge of the nobility and grace of the Greek forms, and that he accomplished this by executing all his earlier and more important compositions in strict accordance with the severe requirement of classic taste. To his influence, more than to that of any other individual, is the French school of to-day indebted not only for its existence, but for the excellence of its teaching as well. The success of his efforts stimulated such men as Gros, Girard, Girodet, Coignet, Flandrin, Delaroche, and others, to work on his lines, and through them came down to the time of Couture, in a stream of unbroken continuity, the influence of the founder's teaching which fittingly culminated in Thomas Couture's immortal work, "The Decadence of the Roman Empire." This beyond all doubt is the most comprehensive and completely artistic composition that the brush of a painter belonging to our times has given us. The composition, epitomizing as it does an important period in the history of the greatest nation of antiquity, the correct drawing and suggestive grouping of the numerous figures, the warmth and richness of color, tell the well-known story of debauchery and dissipation, sapping the physical vitality and destroying the *morale* of a great people, as it was never told before. With the birth of this noble work there died nearly all that was left of the positively Greek influence, which for nearly a hundred years had been such an important factor in the development of the French school of painting.

BREAKING AWAY FROM CLASSIC INFLUENCE.

While the gradual decline of classic influence was going on, running *pari passu* with it was an evolution of something new, which in the end was destined to give wide scope to individual effort, and to lessen the purely academic force of the circumscribed teaching of the school. The restive spirit of the nineteenth century had sown its seed, and in due time a harvest of new men was ripening—men who displayed great technical skill and talent for new styles of composition. Many of them, after the years of academic drudgery were passed, abandoned the traditions of the school, started out upon fresh lines, and created what might almost be denominated new fashions in art. Their work soon assumed a highly decorative form; subjects were selected with special reference to telling or pleasing situations, which afforded opportunities for the display of very decorative schemes of color. For nearly half a century the only notably outstanding exception to this rule was in the work of a few artists, who formed what is now known as the "Barbazon school." The men constituting this little band of earnest workers were artists in the truest sense of that much abused term. They pursued the more conservative course, and confined their efforts to delineating in a marvelously truthful, striking, and often poetic way, such choice bits of nature as only those possessing the art instinct most highly developed could discover and portray.

From what has been written the inference will be rightly drawn that, in the belief of the writer, there exists in France a national school of art technique, such as no other nation can show. It seems necessary to set forth some of the reasons or facts upon which this opinion is based.

THE SYSTEM OF ART EDUCATION IN FRANCE.

The most important set of facts upon which this conclusion rests, relates to the connection of the Government with the art education of the French people. Coupled with the State Department of Public Instruction is that of the Fine Arts. The member of the cabinet who directs these departments is accordingly styled : "*Ministre de l'Instruction Publique et des Beaux Arts.*" This functionary has under his control all the national museums in France. To him are referred all propositions for the purchase of works of art from the public funds for the collections in different cities. Models for statues and designs for public buildings, together with the interior decoration of these last, have to be approved by him. Librarians, directors, curators, keepers of prints, and all experts who have to do with the artistic and antiquarian collections belonging to the public, are appointed by him, and it is to the credit of these ministers, who have existed from the time of Louis XIV, that their appointments in connection with the arts have usually been made with special reference to the fitness of persons for the duties they had to fulfill. It is assumed in government circles that only a long course of special training can prepare a man for the responsible position of director of a great collection, and this business has been so arranged that there is always a competent and acceptable expert ready at hand, who can at a moment's notice fill any important vacancy that may occur. One of the results of this perfect system is that no country in the world can present a longer line of illustrious men who have created and presided over great collections than France. These officials are held in high esteem, honored with many marks of distinction, well paid, and pensioned when their days of usefulness are over. In France there is no national quality more clearly apparent than respect for the arts and works of all kinds connected with them. This trait belongs to no condition nor class, but pervades alike all ranks of society. There, as in other countries, the fame of the average politician is usually short-lived : but the protectors of the arts build monuments which keep their names remembered, because they have delighted and instructed thousands of their fellowmen.

STATE ENCOURAGEMENT TO STUDENTS AND ARTISTS.

Another important element to be considered in relation to this subject is the direct and substantial encouragement which not only natives but foreigners studying in France receive from the Government. The spirit of the French people is so broad and catholic in all matters pertaining to art that they make but little distinction between the productions of native and foreign artists, and the consequence is, that the works of living men of many nationalities may be seen, hanging side by side with those of natives, in all museums and exhibitions to which contemporary art is admitted.

The national budget of each year contains a liberal appropriation for the purchase of works of art and for the proper maintenance of the national collections. From this fund annual purchases are made, chiefly from the works exhibited at the *salon*, and these are distributed among the galleries of the different cities. In each distribution, little distinction is made between the national collections and those under the control of and owned by the municipalities. These last are often enriched by important gifts from the Government.

The artists appreciating this national recognition, and the advantages of the encouragement they receive, in a spirit of reciprocity frequently accept comparatively low prices for their better works when purchased for the public galleries. That their works should have been found worthy of such distinctive recognition is regarded by them as an especial honor. In no other country is the *entente cordiale* between government officials and artists so complete. The former recognize the value of the arts as one of the most important elements of success in the great combination of social and political forces which has come to be known as modern civilization, and the latter, heartily responding to this enlightened recognition, exhibit an honest pride in working for the promotion of a nation's refinement.

SCHOOL OF PAINTING.

Of late so much has been said and written about the superiority of the "French school" over all others of these later times, and its popular, artistic, and commercial success being well assured, a brief inquiry into its exact status appears to be necessary here, for the purpose of ascertaining if in reality it has an actual existence, i. e., in the ancient or any other acceptation of the term "school of painting."

When an author cites the school of Bellini, Mantegna, Da Vinci, or Titian, the reader who is at all versed in the history of Italian art comprehends the exact meaning of the expression. which in its broadest signification has a rather narrow application, and refers usually to the pupils (and imitators) of this or that master, when they were numerous enough to be called a school and followed the method and style of their teacher. In the days of the early Italian painters there were no academies with a corps of professors for teaching the arts, and probably for that reason the master became, as it were, a school by himself, and his pupils and their followers maintained the technical traditions of the particular studio.

We also know what is meant by the term "Venetian school." The visitor to Venice, enchanted by the richness of color, and the rare nobility and grace of form which greet him in every public building, church, and palace, does not usually stop to ask the name of the artist whose imagination gave birth to this or that exquisite composition, but contents himself with the fact that he is in the actual presence of one of the great and fascinating masterpieces of the "Venetian school;" and not only the individual, but the civilized part of the world, acknowledges the force and art value of this comprehensive expression. Neither recorded nor existing facts warrant the conclusion that any single French artist living within the last half of the century has been the founder of his own or the promoter of any other school of art. The demands of the times do not encourage imitations. Students are now taught the elements or the handiwork of their calling, rather than how to paint pictures in a particular manner. The best imitations meet with but little encouragement, while often poor original work brings unexpected approbation, not only from the amateur but from the man of commerce. The fortunate want of demand for imitative work has completely done away with the necessity for the individual school, and hence it is that we never hear of the school of Couture, of Meissonnier, of Gerome, or of Bonnat. It is greatly to the credit of these, and many others of the later French masters, that they have never attempted to hamper the breadth of their teaching by the narrowing boundaries of a school.

Since the Dusseldorf days there has been no concentrated attempt to found a school of art, and that attempt ; after a few years of nominal success, turned out to be such a failure that its history has no doubt prevented artists in other countries from repeating such an experiment.

The school at Munich still exists, and continues to receive and instruct students, but its success over its older rival consists chiefly in the fact of its having lasted longer, rather than its proved capacity to make artists.

A few years ago there appeared a small circle of enthusiasts who were given to the worship of unearthly and strange things. They called themselves "Impressionists," and labored under the impression that they had found a new key with which to unlock the secrets of nature, and a new route to fame. They told their little circumference in the world that they had discovered something new and had founded a school ; but the greater world refused to listen or believe, and their bantling still languishes in the swaddling clothes of a fruitless attempt.

THE ÉCOLE DES BEAUX ARTS.

Notwithstanding the fact that there does not exist in France a school of art in the popular acceptation of the term, there is a source of knowledge—a place for teaching all that can be taught in the way of certain rules—and it is known as the "École des Beaux Arts,"* and was under the control of the "Académie des Beaux Arts," and is now indirectly under the direction of the Government. It generously receives from all quarters of the globe those who would cultivate a knowledge of the arts. Formerly examinations for admission were rather superficial, and were seemingly made with special reference to granting easy access. Now, however, owing to the prospective crowding out of natives by a great and ever-increasing influx of foreigners, they have become more comprehensive and exacting; not more so, however, than they ought to be to prevent the waste of valuable time bestowed in teaching the simplest rudiments. The examination passed successfully, and without any payment, the student enters his class and becomes entitled to all the privileges and advantages of the academy. He may continue his studies for an unlimited period, as there is no particular time prescribed for them or regular course insisted upon.

Students upon entering choose their course of instruction either in painting, sculpture, or architecture. In all of these branches the best teachers available are appointed to instruct, and they, as a rule, visit their classes for a short time each day, for the purpose of inspecting and correcting the work of the pupils. The instructors who accept these appointments are acknowledged masters, and are usually among the most successful in their respective branches. They must make a great sacrifice by undertaking these duties, which compel them to devote a considerable portion of their time to an occupation for which they receive no adequate compensation. This remarkable evidence of *esprit de corps* may be accepted as conclusive proof that those who pursue the arts in France are possessed of great love for the higher interests of their vocation.

COURSE OF STUDIES.

The studies at the "École des Beaux Arts" are divided, as already indicated, into three sections. These are:

1. *Section of painting.*—In this is included instruction in engraving upon metals and etching. The students must draw from nature and the antique, and copy from selected old masters: they must also study anatomy, perspective, archæology, costume, modeling, elementary architecture, geology, physics, general chemistry, and especially the chemistry of colors.

2. *Section of sculpture.*—In this section the art of engraving upon

---

* There are in Paris several private art schools for painting and sculpture, which in their teaching as to *technique* cover the field occupied by Government institutions. The most successful and better known of these is called "the Julian," after the name of its director, M. Randolph Julian. This is a well-organized school, and possesses every facility for a thorough course of technical instruction. Among its masters are to be found some of the best known teachers, and the fees are moderate.

metals and precious stones, is also taught, and, with the exception of modeling from nature and the antique, the general course of study is about the same as in the section of painting.

3. *Section of architecture.*—This is the most extended and comprehensive of the three courses, and embraces the study of various sciences, including mathematics, descriptive geometry, stereotomy, perspective, construction, ancient architecture, drawing working plans, sketching from fragments, from nature, and the antique. In connection with each section there is an extensive course of literature, and a series of special lectures, historical and technical, is given, applicable to each order of study, and free of charge. Besides the direct teaching of masters, the pupils of all the sections may copy and read at will in all the galleries, museums, and extensive art library attached to the school.

HISTORY OF THE ÉCOLE DES BEAUX ARTS.

In 1635 Richelieu instituted the "Académie Française," and in 1648 the foundation of the "École des Beaux Arts" was laid. It was then called the "*Académie Royale de Peinture et de Sculpture.*" That year was made famous by the peace of Westphalia, which put an end to the Thirty Years' War, and five years after the boy king, Louis, had succeeded his father to the throne of France. In 1661 the king appointed the great Colbert his *Contrôleur-Général,* who within a few years instituted the "*Académie des Sciences,*" the "*Académie des Inscriptions et Belles-Letters*" and the "*Académie d'Architecture.*" He also reformed the "*Académie de Peinture.*" which up to his time had been an association for the cultivation of the arts rather than a school. He moreover established the French school at Rome as an adjunct to the Paris school, and this was the origin of the now much coveted "*Grand Prix de Rome,*" given annually to three or four French students of marked ability, and which enables them to continue their studies for four years (engravers three years) at Rome, at the expense of the state. From the reign of Louis XIV to the revolution, the School of Fine Arts existed without interruption, and during the whole of that period was useful in promoting a practical knowledge of the beautiful.

THE CLOSING OF THE SCHOOL.

In 1793 the wild spirits who controlled the affairs of France arrived at the conclusion that the nation had greater need of guillotines than pictures and statues. In that year the Abbé Gregoire read a report before the convention proposing the suppression of the "*École des Beaux Arts.*" The convention accepted the reporter's conclusions, and the school was closed. Matters remained in this state for two decades, and it was not until the first years of the restoration had passed that the usefulness of the school was again fully realized. It should be mentioned, however, that Napoleon had authorized a limited course of art instruction at the expense of the state. Nevertheless it remained for the Bourbons to revise and reorganize the school. This was done by royal decree in 1818. In 1819 Minister Decaze promulgated a statute which placed the institution upon its present broad and comprehensive foundation. It organized the studies, assigned the locality for the building, appointed professors,s and placed it under the direction of the "*Académie des Beaux Arts.*" Later came Louis Philippe and Louis Napoleon, both of whom were active promoters of the arts and sciences, and each took an especial interest in the improvement and efficiency of the National School of Arts. During their reigns many beneficent measures were adopted. In 1864 the organization reached its culminating point upon the issue of a decree establishing definitely the course of the studies, detaching the school from the "*Académie des Beaux Arts,*" and placing it under an independent administration, with a special director at its head.

THE INSTITUTE OF FRANCE.

L'Institut de France, as now constituted, is composed of five academies, viz: the "*Académie Française,*" the "*Académie des Inscriptions et Belles-Lettres,*" the "*Académie des Sciences,*" the "*Académie des Beaux Arts,*" and the "*Académie des Sciences Morales et Politiques.*" It is acknowledged throughout the world to be a most effective agency for the dissemination of learning. It is not only the center of all that is best in French civilization, but its influence is felt wherever the education and development of the human mind are appreciated. No great achievement is too far off to be beyond its recognition. Its portals are wide open to all the earnest students of the universe. The scientist and the artist receive the same warm welcome from whatever quarter of the globe they may come. The Institute of France is the chief glory of the French nation.

It speaks eloquently for the character of this people that they have so realized the civilizing value of all of the arts, and it is also creditable to their past rulers who, acting upon a proper and intelligent appreciation of national sentiment, inaugurated and caused to be maintained such perfect means for the cultivation of artistic taste.

PROVINCIAL SCHOOLS OF ART.

The leading provincial schools of art which are efficient and thoroughly well organized should be briefly noticed in order to render the exposition of fine art organization in France more complete. These in the alphabetical order of the cities are:

AMIENS.—The Provincial Fine Art School of the city of Amiens. The course of instruction is as follows: (1) Elementary drawing;

(2) modeling; (3) anatomy, applied to fine art; (4) imitation drawing (relievo and nature); (5) mathematics; (6) lineal drawing; (7) drawing classes for young girls; (8) history of art.

BORDEAUX.—Municipal School of Drawing, Painting, and Architecture of the City of Bordeaux: (1) Imitation drawing; (2) figure painting and history; (3) drawing and ornament painting; (4) lineal drawing; (5) perspective; (6) anatomy and physiology applied to the art of drawing; (7) architecture; (8) mathematical and physical science applied to architecture; (9) history of art.

BOURGES.—National School of Fine Arts at Bourges: (1) Lineal and geometrical drawing; (2) architectural drawing, mathematics, construction, and perspective; (3) ornamental designing, figure drawing, and composition; (4) architecture; (5) sculpture; (6) painting; (7) painting and sculpture applied to ceramics; (8) anatomy; (9) history of art.

CALAIS.—School of Decorative and Industrial Art of St. Pierre-les-Calais: (1) The classical study of drawing up to and including the knowledge required to obtain the diploma of capability to teach drawing in the university schools; (2) the study of anatomy; (3) the application of the art of drawing to the different professions and industries; (4) the professional application of all the arts to various purposes.

DIJON.—National School of Fine Arts at Dijon: (1) Drawing (lineal and ornamental) from the rudiments up to and comprising composition; (2) figure drawing and painting; (3) sculpture; (4) architecture; (5) perspective; (6) anatomy; (7) history of art; (8) elementary geometry and descriptive geometry; (9) stereotomy; (10) frame and mechanical tracings; (11) industrial drawing.

LILLE.—Academical schools of the city of Lille: (1) Lineal drawing; (2) drawing of figures and ornaments; (3) drawing of plastic or models; (4) painting and composition; (5) anatomy; (6) perspective; (7) geometry applied to arts and elements of mechanics; (8) elementary architecture; (9) normal teaching of drawing.

LYONS.—The city of Lyons possesses, in addition to a National School of Fine Arts, drawing schools under the direct control of the municipality. At the National School the courses are as follows: (1) The drawing of figures, flowers, up to and including composition; (2) painting; (3) sculpture; (4) architecture; (5) engraving and lithography; (6) anatomy and physiology of forms applied to the fine arts; (7) history of art and the elements of archæology; (8) practical geometry, descriptive geometry, stereotomy, and perspective.

There are seven municipal schools, viz: Five for boys and male adults, one for young girls, and a drawing and painting school for ladies.

MARSEILLES.—The School of Fine Arts at Marseilles: (1) Elementary drawing of the figure; (2) figure drawing from antique plasters; (3) drawing and modeling from life; (4) sculpture; (5) architecture.

MONTPELLIER.—Provincial School of Fine Arts at Montpellier: (1) Study of the living model for painting and drawing; (2) drawing after the antique in round relievo; (3) elementary figure drawing; (4) sculpture; (5) drawing of ornaments, architectural and industrial drawing; (6) stereotomy; (7) history of art; (8) perspective; (9) anatomy.

NANCY.—Municipal and Provincial School of Fine Arts at Nancy: (1) Lineal drawing and geometry; (2) perspective; (3) elements of architecture; (4) drawing; (5) modeling; (6) comparative anatomy; (7) composition of ornaments; (8) history of art; (9) oil painting; (10) painting in water colors; (11) normal courses for students wishing to learn drawing.

NICE.—National School of Decorative Art at Nice: (1) Lineal and geometrical drawing; (2) surveying; (3) leveling; (4) architecture; (5) construction; (6) mathematics; (7) perspective; (8) stereotomy; (9) anatomy; (10) painting; (11) sculpture.

ROUEN.—Provincial School of Fine Arts at Rouen: (1) Classical study of drawing; (2) painting; (3) sculpture; (4) application of drawing to industry; (5) history of art.

ST. ETIENNE.—Provincial School of Industrial Arts at St. Etienne. The teaching in this school is divided into elementary, middle, and superior drawing. The special courses are: (1) Elementary geometry; (2) descriptive geometry; (3) perspective; (4) anatomy; (5) history of decorative art; (6) physics and chemistry; (7) geometrical drawing.

TURCOING.—Academical (Free) School at Turcoing: (1) Drawing; (2) painting; (3) decorative art; (4) architecture; (5) plastic studies and modeling; (6) history of art.

TOULOUSE.—Municipal School of Fine Arts and Industrial Science at Toulouse. The school of Toulouse is one of the oldest and best organized in France. The city has a celebrated connection with the arts. The first public school for the study of the nude was established in 1726. In 1750 it was made a Royal Academy of Painting, Sculpture, and Architecture, by Louis XV. The National Convention in 1793 suppressed the title of "Royal Academy," but the school remained. The principles on which the instruction is regulated are much the same as they were at the time of the revolution. The school teaches everything appertaining to painting, sculpture, and architecture, and it sends every year its best pupils to continue their studies at the *Ecole des Beaux Arts* in Paris.

VALENCIENNES.—Communal Academy of Drawing, Painting, Sculpture, and Architecture at Valenciennes. The academy proper is composed of the leading artists of the city. At the school in con-

FINE ARTS.   31

nection with it are taught drawing and modeling, and their application to the different professions and industries. The academy
also prepares professors of drawing for the universities and municipal schools.

ALGIERS.

There is an important National School of Fine Arts at Algiers.
It teaches: (1) Geometrical lineal drawing and perspective; (2) ornamental drawing, history, and composition of ornaments; (3) figure
drawing and anatomy; (4) architecture, mathematics, and construction; (5) painting; (6) sculpture; (7) history of art and archæology;
(8) application of drawing to industries.

FRENCH NATIONAL MANUFACTURES.

The French national manufactures—those which are under state
control and direction—are intimately associated with the history of
art in France. The results which they have achieved are such as any
nation might regard with peculiar pride. It is not surprising then
that Sèvres porcelain and Gobelins and Beauvais tapestry should have
been given a conspicuous place in the Exhibition of 1889. The most
important of these fine art manufactures have, after a long period of
state protection and an enormous expenditure of public money,
been brought to such excellence that it is difficult to conceive how
they can be made to reach any higher degree of perfection. Nevertheless the endeavor to attain something still higher is as strong
now as it was a hundred years ago. It is an amazing fact that, notwithstanding all the convulsions through which France has passed
in modern times, each successive régime has realized the importance
of maintaining these manufactures, and that although they are a
legacy of the old monarchy they have never been made to suffer
by political fanaticism. The following grants figure annually in
the French budget: Sèvres, 624,450 francs; les Gobelins, 231,520
francs; Beauvais, 116,350 francs; Mosaics, 25,000 francs. Only a
small portion of this money returns to the exchequer from the limited
sales which are sanctioned by the Government. All the really important works of art produced at the manufactories are used for
decorating public buildings in France, or as the state gifts to the
heads of foreign nations, distinguished visitors, and others.

GOBELINS.

The Gobelins manufactory originated in the middle of the fifteenth
century, when Jean Gobelins, a dyer of Rheims, settled on the banks
of the Bièvre, near Paris, and made a reputation by his dyes. Gobelins' industry became afterward combined with that of tapestry
weaving on the spot that he had chosen for his workshop, and there
was a considerable establishment here in the seventeenth century

when Louis XIV made it a " Royal Manufactory of Crown Uphol-
stery." In 1667 it was under the direction of the painter Lebrun, and
for some years it was used for the manufacture of various furniture.
It was closed for a time, and when it was reopened in 1699, the
Gobelins and the adjoining Savonnerie only produced tapestries and
carpets. The regulations of the Gobelins manufactory have been
revised since 1871. The establishment is now composed of a manufactory proper, a school of tapestry, and a dyeing school. The
workmen are all trained on the premises. They enter as boys, and
go through a long apprenticeship. In connection with the tapestry
weaving these workmen may very properly be termed artists.

BEAUVAIS.

The history of the Beauvais manufactory does not go back so far
as that of the Gobelins. It was founded in 1667 by Louis Hinart, a
tapestry weaver from Paris, and began to flourish ten years later
under the direction of Philippe Behacle, a native of Flanders. Like
the Gobelins, it subsequently became raised to the rank of a state
manufactory. Besides its school of tapestry, it has its drawing
school. The important technical distinction between Gobelins and
Beauvais tapestry is that the former is high-warp while the latter is
low-warp.

SÈVRES.

The history of the Sèvres manufactory is, briefly, as follows: A
royal porcelain factory was established at Vincennes in 1740, a
previous experiment having been made at St. Cloud at the close of
the previous century. In 1756 the royal factory was transferred
from Vincennes to Sèvres, where it has since remained. Its general
organization is very similar to that of the Gobelins and Beauvais
manufactories. In addition to its workshop it has its practical school
where the workmen or artists are trained from early youth. Only
Frenchmen are employed in the establishment, but foreigners can
study in the school if they are properly recommended. It is the
custom to choose the regular apprentices from among the children
of the workmen, so that the art may be said to descend from father
to son. The studies in the primary school last two years, and those
in the special school five years. The primary lessons comprise lineal
drawing and geometry, ornament drawing, drawing of bas-reliefs,
perspective, and elementary lessons in modeling. The special school
teaches in addition to advanced geometrical drawing and perspective, the elements of architecture, modeling from living plants, etc.,
composition and coloring, and the principles of decorative art.

MOSAIC MANUFACTORY.

Although Francis I brought workers in mosaic from Italy into
France, he did not found any school for the perpetuation of this art

on French soil. The National Manufactory of Mosaics is of quite recent origin, for it dates only from 1876. One of the chief reasons for its establishment was the restoration of mosaics belonging to the state. There is a school attached to it.

LANDSCAPE PAINTING.

It is probable that no nation has produced so many landscape painters as France, and yet it can not be said that from the time of Claude to the present day there has ever existed, in a broad sense of the term, a-school of French landscape painting. Nothing that has occurred of late years lessens the force of this assertion. Each epoch in the art history of the country has produced its series of good landscape masters; but they have passed along in lines rather than by groups, and their individual influence has often died with them. To-day there are two or three recognized leaders, each standing quite as much by himself as any of his predecessors. No two living French landscape painters appear to see nature alike, judging from the distinct manner in which they treat it on canvas. This indicates individuality, but not necessarily individuality in its better sense, for a sameness of purpose is perceptible in nearly every work. The majority of landscapists possess sufficient facility for copying nature correctly to make their works objects of interest, especially when the scenes selected are picturesque; but as a rule they only convey to the minds of others the outside of nature. Their pictures are not generally suggestive, and the deeper sentiments with which grand and lovely scenes inspire those who have vivid imaginations are not often found in the works of the later French landscape painters.

It must be admitted that great judgment is often displayed in the choice of scenes, and that in transferring these to canvas the way in which the mechanics of art are employed leaves little to be desired. The painting is often free and the delineation of rock surfaces, details of trees, mountain forms, sky reflections in water, cloud effects, light and shadow, architectural details, etc., are as true to the reality as possible. But notwithstanding all this excellent *technique*, there is usually something wanting that is undefinable. The realism is perfect; what is lacking is related to the unreal, or rather, the ideal. It is soul that we miss—a subtle something that touches the feelings and takes the reflective mind below the mere surface of things. When this quality is absent we know that the artist has been manufactured. Schools may develop the art instinct, but they can not create it

The majority of French artists, like those of other nationalities, do not exhibit an exact appreciation of the value of correct ærial perspective, a quality in landscape art which has so much to do with regulating distances, throwing back the horizon line, in a word, giving to a composition the true atmospheric effect of out-

H. Ex. 410—VOL 2——3

door scenes. It appears to be an essential in art which can not be taught by rules.

The landscapes in the French part of the Exhibition are often thoroughly representative of contemporary work, and are well worthy of consideration on account of their truthful expression of various phases of nature. There are many ambitious and serious paintings which convey to the mind all the ideas of nature which accomplished *technique* is capable of communicating. In several notable instances enough of the ideal is expressed to excite the admiration of the cultivated and critical.

Of the fifty-two living landscape painters represented, Cazin assuredly stands near the first. His works possess the indescribable charm already alluded to. Transparency of color, simplicity of composition, dignity of form, brilliant quality of light and air, these and other essentials are strikingly present in them. He also possesses an apt sense of the picturesque and a rare talent for expressing unity of purpose. His creations never fail to be daintily artistic, but his figures are not generally successful, and his works would be better without them.

The refined works of Raphael Collin are wonderfully spiritual, and rise far above the bare realities of nature, and are delicate and imaginative to a poetic degree. Harpignies is true to nature, and there is more charm in his skies and atmospheric effects than in those of most of his *confréres*, who are disposed to copy strictly what they see. His trees are most carefully drawn, and express with great fidelity peculiarities of foliage, barks, etc.

Busson is a close copyist of commonplace scenes, which are not usually interesting. The large works of Binet are composed in a serious spirit, and commonly show breadth of treatment, harmony of design, and express somewhat of the poetic. Zuber's works are particularly strong, and well conceived. He never shows a weak canvas, or one that does not fix the attention. Seriousness of purpose, and great technical skill are the chief characteristics of his productions. Heilbuth's pictures are invariably charming. The great master of earthy realism is Pelouse. His painted trees, rocks, shrubs, grasses, and mosses are marvels in their way, and it may be said that no artist has ever carried literal copying from nature to such perfection as he. His imitations are like realities. The directness and wonderful fidelity of his art are entitled to the respect of those who admire honesty of purpose and truthfulness. There are other landscape painters who do good work, but their creations, as a rule, rise only to a moderate standard of merit. Fairly good landscapes, however, have no great value, and for this reason it is not necessary to mention the names of those who paint them.

PORTRAIT: PUVIS DE CHAVANNES, BY BONNAT.

PORTRAITURE.

France, like other countries, can not boast of having many artists who produce portraits of great excellence. Of the sixty-two who exhibit specimens of their work during the last ten years, it would be difficult to discover half a dozen who show anything above the uninteresting level of commonplace. The majority of them seem to plod on upon the same old lines which have been followed in all countries for at least the last fifty years. The ordinary portrait shows a well dressed person, whose attitude plainly indicates that he or she has been posed for a "picture." The eyes are always staring the beholder out of countenance; each particular hair, crease of clothing, peculiarity of cravat, ribbon, knot, ruff, tuck, and frill, is represented with the utmost fidelity. All details with regard to chairs, tables, windows, etc., are not less rigidly preserved. It is such stiff and artificial work, turned out by 95 per cent. of the portrait painters of the last half century, that has contributed to enlarge the private art collections of the entire world. Had it not been for the existence of a small number of strong and original workers, portrait painting would long ago have been counted among the dead arts. France to-day possesses at least one such painter, whose work is free from all tricks of trade. It is faithful to the great object and end of portrait painting, which is the pictorial reproduction of the individual in his everyday mood, the one that more fully expresses all that distinguishes that person from all others. It is the faculty of transferring the ruling characteristics of the individual to canvas that proves the greatness of the artist. Durer and Holbein stand very prominently among the great masters who possessed the talent of catching the natural average expression, and the character of the individual with it. The French artist of to-day who has that faculty to a much greater degree than any other among his countrymen is Bonnat. If his portraits at the Exhibition prove one thing more than another, it is that he paints the moral and intellectual, as well as the physical. Of the nine he exhibits, the wonderful portrait of Puvis de Chavannes stands out conspicuously by its many excellencies. It will for all time hold its own as one of the best examples of portraiture which this century has produced. Color, pose, drawing, and expression tell the story of the man just as he is, naught extenuated nor set down in frivolity; but the true man, in all his honesty, frankness, and well-bred charming simplicity of manner, is placed upon the canvas. Here we have the distinguished artist from every point of view. The portrait of Victor Hugo shows the same directness and intelligence of purpose. Not less remarkable is the charmingly composed portrait of Pasteur and his little niece, wherein we see the scientific benefactor of the human race with his protecting arm over helpless and confiding childhood. Here again the face

plainly reveals the refined and benevolent character of the studious
man, who is devoting his life to the grand ideal of improving the
condition of his kind. Between the portraits of Hugo and Pasteur
there hangs, in all the ostentation of the rich colors and ample folds
of ecclesiastical vestments, the portrait of Cardinal Lavigerie. Again
we see the character of the man, or rather the man-created official of
the creator. His position in the chair where he sits, and his facial
expression bespeak the ecclesiastic, proud in authority—a single cog
of a wheel is the most earthy of all earthy machines. A portrait bust
of the younger Dumas is quite as remarkable for its many fine qualities as the other works mentioned. It would be superfluous to attempt further description of the works of this great artist. They now
assert their rightful position in the history of contemporary art, and
assuredly will stand the test of time.

Gervex, in his portrait of Alfred Stevens, shows a fine feeling for
simplicity in composition and directness of aim. His large canvas
of the members of the Salon Jury of Painters, is a most interesting
collection of portraits, and it brings the life and movement of a well-
known yearly scene vividly before the spectator. The grouping is
natural and excellent. Roll, in his portraits of Alphand and Demoye,
both done with a free hand, displays rare facility of execution and
a most happy conception of the true end of portrait painting. Dupain
contributes a good specimen of his faithfully elaborated and ornate
work. His portrait of Admiral Mouchey is one of the best examples
of this particular kind of art in the whole Exhibition. A portrait
of Edmond de Goncourt, by Raffaelli, is exceedingly lifelike and
striking. The color has a certain chalkiness, which some artists
would call "snappy." The work is strongly composed, but it goes
a little too near the crudities of the Impressionists to be pleasing to
the eye, and the whole scheme of color suggests *post-mortem* conditions.

But the ultraimpressionist portraits of the Exhibition are those
of two ladies by Besnard. They fairly out-Herod Herod, and effectually put into the background the lower toned works of Manet. In
the luridness of their prismatic color they are far enough away from
nature to represent supernatural objects. Is not their effectiveness,
of which there can be no doubt, merely affectation? Such work may
represent the art of the future. But let us hope, however, that this
future is still very far off.

Carolus-Duran exhibits eight portraits. One, " Mme. la Comtesse
V." is a dignified, earnest work, strong in color. The pose of the
figure is natural, and the likeness is probably a faithful one. This
portrait must be regarded as one of his best of the present time. The
others are only performances of his average merit. They show fine
technical work in the painting of stuffs, and skill in posing and the
graceful arrangement of the draperies, but they are rather disap-

pointing, and do not seem to reach the standard which we have a right to expect from the brush of so good an artist.

There are two portraits by Meissonnier, one of a young lady and the other of himself. The latter is dated 1889, and is one of the latest works from his easel. It is so new and original in its treatment, that it stands quite by itself. The costume is suggestive of a priest's *soutane;* but the color is of light terra cotta, and the garment opens and fastens down the front. The head, costume, and the surroundings suggest the period of the *Rennaissance* vividly, so well is the ancient style portrayed, and the likeness is a faithful one. The pose is dignified, easy, and natural. No doubt the artist painted this portrait with the idea that it would be the one by which he would be known in the future. None could answer that purpose better.

FIGURE PAINTING.

Of the compositions exhibited whose claim to merit rests chiefly upon the study of the human figure there is much to be said, and more to praise than in condemnation. The professional critic, who writes so knowingly and with such an air of absolute authority, consigning with a scratch of the pen to his own particular oblivion, a work that may have cost its creator months and perhaps years of patient labor, knows practically nothing of the great difficulties involved in the production upon canvas of an acceptable representation of the human form. It is, of all the great essentials in art, the one for which the ambitious painter has the most frequent use, and is at the same time the most difficult to master, and unless he can present it in a fairly truthful way, his compositions, wherein the human figure occurs, although they may possess certain elements of success, can not be acceptable to those capable of discriminating the false from the true.

To a certain point of mechanical correctness only is about as far as the average modern figure painter ever gets. We may take academic correctness as the present standard, and admit those who have reached it to be worthy of consideration. The writer feels that the exquisite grace which Raphael knew how to portray, and the grandeur of the male human form which Michael Angelo painted are no longer attainable. If such is the case, we must take the best we have and make the most of it, nor bestow wholesale condemnation upon earnest workers because they can not reach the highest standards raised by the greatest artists of all time.

Prominent among the figure painters of the present day is Benjamin Constant, who exhibits ten works, seven of which, in his well-known style of coloring, are full of his individuality, and are not by any possibility to be mistaken for those of any other artist. The work of this painter may not be of the highest order, but it is at least his own, and is not to be easily imitated. The other compositions are decorative pieces, occupying three panels, and intended for the council hall of the Sorbonne. They are entitled "Les Lettres," "L'Académie de Paris," "Les Sciences." These are in the purely decorative style now in vogue, both as regards color and composition, and are quite worthy of the position they are destined to occupy.

Jean Beraud is another among the representative painters who have created something new, which may be called their own. His most important work, among the four exhibited, is entitled "A la Salle Graffard." It represents a meeting of Anarchists who wish to reform the world down to their own level. The scene is exciting and s vividly portrayed. The expressions of the leaders' faces are such that the work might be described as a conference of the Infernals. The artist seems to have painted without exaggeration an actual scene.

P. Albert Besnard is more than half way on the road to the Impressionist goal. The great difference between his work and that of other Impressionists is this, that his is full of original suggestion ; but at its best it is not far removed from the drop curtain of a spectacular drama, painted by one of the better scenic artists. This kind of painting is like a certain kind of so-called music, it needs explanation.

A. William Bouguereau contributes ten works, the most important as to size and the number of figures in the composition being *·Jeunesse de Bacchus."* The scheme of color is that which has come to be associated with this artist. The women are pale pink, the men dark brown. The drawing of the figures is (academically) remarkably good; that of the man in the foreground being especially strong. The work shows throughout the evidence of Greek culture; and although there is a great deal of correct nudity in it, and the subject lends itself to voluptuous treatment, there is no impure suggestion. Refinement is one of the ruling qualities of M. Bouguereau's works. but it is apt to become insipid. His next important subject is *"Jésus Christ rencontre sa mère."* The Christ is conventional; the mother is outlined with academical correctness; but the picture leaves no impression of creative thought. Of the other eight pictures, several are very beautiful from their soft harmony of color and purity of line. The works of this artist, although they are so devoid of the emotional, have an undeniable charm that appeals to many. They are probably destined to occupy a prominent place in the history of French art of the nineteenth century.

M. Jules Breton is a painter of the French peasant. He has given the world a greater variety of truthful pictures of the peasants' everyday life than any other artist. He has represented his rustics as rather intelligent beings, not half idiotic, in the manner of Millet. We see them in every phase of their habitual existence, but they are always men and women who seem to enter upon their labors, devotions, and amusements like the rest of humanity. If the art of this painter has exercised any influence upon those who have contemplated his works, it has been to raise the peasant in their estimation while Millet's rustics may excite pity in the breasts of a few, the brutality and coarseness of the types disgust the majority. Among the works by Jules Breton contributed to this Exhibition is to be seen the sketch of "*Le soir dans les hameaux du Finistère*," which the writer regards as his most artistic composition. The others bear the stamp of an earnest and intelligent worker, who has labored in a field open to all, and who has made it in some respects peculiarly his own; but in his later works there seems to be a falling off from the strength of his former days.

Pascal A. J. Dagnan-Bouveret has received the highest recompense at the Paris Salon of 1889, and also the medal of honor from the International Art Jury of the Exhibition. It has been said of him that he is the coming man, but if the obtaining of two of the highest official recognitions for his work in one year signifies anything, he has already come. His work, like those of nearly all the great masters, is remarkable for solidity, careful drawing, and great attention to detail. It is as far off from the Impressionist methods as daylight is from darkness, and offers not the slightest indication of that supposed *abandon* which painters of questionable knowledge often have recourse to for the purpose of producing a sort of slapdash effect, which tickles the appetite of the inexperienced buyer, and which the dealer knows how to turn to account. His work, which received the first prize at the salon, is in every respect most carefully executed. The grouping of the figures is picturesque, and the pose of each is natural and unconstrained. The lines of the drapery are easy, and the textures are correctly painted, but not overwrought, so as to make them an ostentatious feature. Sky, landscape, and atmosphere are painted with skill betraying perfect knowledge of values. The whole composition is conservative, and one may search in vain for a single touch of the brush that was not made with an intelligent purpose. The sterling worth of the picture grows upon the mind, and in this respect contrasts strongly with the acres of canvas which bear evidence of "boldness of handling and strong effects of color," in other words, effect of paint, but of nothing beyond. Of M. Dagnan-Bouveret's five pictures at the Exhibition, his "*Pardon*" in Brittany is the most noteworthy.

Of the six works exhibited by Edouard Detaille, "*Le Rêve*" is the most important as to size and subject. It represents a regiment of infantry bivouacked in line of battle with arms stacked. The sleeping soldiers are dreaming of the glories of arms, for in the sky above them is shown a phantom multitude of men bearing arms and flags. The painting is crude, and does not do justice to the artist. His other important work which commands attention is his "*Cossaques de l'Ataman.*" Here we have a regiment of Cossacks on the march. The work is animated, and the column being strung out through the middle distance certainly gives a fair idea of mounted troops in movement; but it is not so good as many of the artist's earlier paintings. The remaining four are also military pieces.

Edouard M. G. Dubufe exhibits four works; two of them large and important, "*Musique Sacrée et Musique Profane,*" diptych, were in the Salon of 1882. These are pleasing and graceful compositions in transparent colors and of a most decorative character, and may be regarded as illustrations of the beautiful in the thoroughly academic style of contemporary art. In the first, angels are singing to the accompaniment of the organ, and in the second groups of nude women in graceful attitudes, are listening to the sensuous strains of a pipe played by a youth. The two works are as opposite in general treatment as possible, but are unmistakably expressive of the ideas intended to be represented. As pictorial efforts they are notable, and among the most attractive in the Exhibition.

Ernest Duez is represented by nine works showing considerable variety of effort. A portrait of the artist Butin, and a small landscape, are the most pleasing of his contributions. The "*Portrait rouge*" does the artist no credit. It is as commonplace as the ordinary illustration in a society novel, and its color is most aggressive. Another work, "*En famille,*" is less offensive in color, but it is conventional, and might have been painted by an artist of inferior ability. This painter, like some others, is particularly mentioned here, less on account of the works he has sent to the Exhibition than because of his well-earned reputation.

Henri Gervex is one of the strongest, boldest, and perhaps the most original among the later French artists. He covers a considerable field in the world of art, and is equally proficient in several departments. His most successful work, composed entirely of portraits, is mentioned elsewhere, but his most startling composition occupies the central place among his nine canvases exhibited, and notwithstanding its peculiarly suggestive character, it justly commands attention. The title of this work is "*Rolla,*" and it depicts a bedroom scene with two figures in it. There is a young woman upon a bed, clothed with flesh tints only, and a man is standing between the bed and a window, evidently puzzled as to what to do—whether to stay or jump out of the window. The composition is the incarnation of deviltry and boldness, the color is brilliant, the whole consummately artistic, and undoubtedly immoral in sentiment. Another of this artist's creations is "*La Femme au Masque,*" a nude woman wearing a little black mask over the upper part of the face. The figure is very gracefully drawn and delicately painted, and altogether the picture is treated with such skill and charm that one does not care to reflect upon the taste shown in the choice of such a subject.

Jean Jacques Henner is represented by eight works; three of his portraits might be colored photographs. Besides these are the well-known pretty head in a red hood, a Christ on the Cross, two of the artist's usual examples of the nude, and a St. Sebastian. The two religious works are interesting, intelligent, and well-executed compositions that do not fall into M. Henner's ordinary groove.

Jean Paul Laurens is the least known in the United States of all the notable French artists of the day. His position among his con-frères is that of the learned student of history and the accomplished painter of serious subjects. With the exception of a portrait now and then, he confines himself to out of the way but interesting incidents. He has the rare faculty of always engaging the attention of those who look at his works. He regards the pursuit of art as an educational occupation, especially as an aid to those who delight in historical research. Two of his works at the Exhibition, "L'Agi-tateur du Languedoc," and "Le Pape et l'Inquisition," may be taken as fine examples of his painting both as regards picturesque compo-sition and choice of subjects.

S. B. Lavastre is represented by a single work, "Frise autour du Dôme Central, au Champ de Mars." It is the composition of a thoroughly educated artist, and is moreover remarkable for the warmth and mellowness of its color, and taken as a whole is one of the great works of this period.

Léon A. Lhermite exhibits two works, "Le Moisson" and "Le Vin." The first is a harvest scene, and the second is the interior of a wine shed, with workmen resting. Both are as realistic as possible, and show no attempt at the picturesque. The men—the principal figures in each picture—are giants, wonderfully drawn. These paint-ings tell nothing save the bare truth, but they tell it strongly.

Albert Maignan is a notable student and a painter whose field is that of historical incidents. His canvases, like those of Laurens, are always interesting. He never chooses a trifling subject, nor tri-fles with it when chosen. His works convey the idea of serious endeavor. Of his eight pictures in the Exhibition "La Voix du Tocsin" is the most remarkable. It tells the story of one of the functions of a church bell. The subject is treated with a vigor of conception and a freedom of physical action seldom equaled. The effect is produced without any exaggeration of the means. Figures seem to have been thrown into the air from the mouth of the bell; and although unsupported, appear to be in their element; others are hanging to the ropes, and they likewise seem to be in their proper places. One is disposed to accept these spirits of the bell as actual entities, so strongly does the imagination of the artist enter into the work. It is a graphic poem upon canvas.

Victor Maree is a painter of rare power, who shows a fine discrimination in the choice of subjects. His three contributions to the Exhibition are most creditable compositions. They do not commend themselves to the crowd, but they appeal to those who look below the surface of a canvas for the deeper significance of the artist's intentions. "*Un lendemain de pays*" tells pathetically and graphically the old, sad story of the helpless, patient wife resigned to her fate, with her frightened children clinging to her for protection, and the brutal, drink-saturated husband in the act of raising a chair to deal the possibly fatal blow. The story of degradation and abject poverty is completely told. Nothing is wanting to convey the cruel lesson belonging to an everyday incident of low life. Can art be put to a better use than that of telling the fortunate their duty towards the unfortunate? Is not the artist who produces a work of this sort a real benefactor to his kind?

J. L. Ernest Meissonier commenced his remarkable career more than fifty years ago; and within the period of the active practice of his calling he has justly achieved the widest artistic reputation of our later times. At the commencement, he marked out the path he intended to follow, and pursued it with singleness of aim until he compelled the universal recognition of his success. Those who are capable of judging, and who know his works, can attest his wonderful skill and truthfulness of execution, and appreciate the difficulties he overcame in producing one of the least important of his carefully wrought compositions. In the absolute perfection of his details, such as the painting of stuffs, leather, metals, feathers, furniture, etc., he has had few, if any, equals. The importance of all these little essentials which go to make a perfect whole is, in his works, never undervalued. Meissonier is also a master of the anatomy of the human figure, and the delineation of facial expression. Whether he depicts the happy repose of the smoker, the vigilant look of the soldier on guard, or the angry and excited movements of men engaged in a quarrel, the expression and action are always natural and suited to the scene. It is greatly to his credit that amid all the temptations by which he has been surrounded he has never deviated from his original direct course, and painted merely for effect. His works have ever been characterized by earnestness of purpose and honest methods. He has always been a l eliever in solidity of painting and careful drawing; constructing intelligently with a view to preserving natural relations; ever seeking simplicity of composition as the highest and noblest attribute of art. Now that he has reached the autumn of his days he has the satisfaction of knowing that honesty of purpose and incessant labor are rewarded with a reputation which rests upon a solid foundation. His fame will stand the test of time; and the luster of his record can not be eclipsed, no matter who may come after him. Moreover, the honors which he has already

FINE ARTS. 43

received have not been empty ones, for there has been bestowed
upon him the most remarkable series of official recognitions ever
awarded to an artist; and the financial appreciation which has flowed
in upon him in a steady stream is without precedent. His ten paintings in the competitive part of the Exhibition, which stand as specimens of his last eleven years' work, excepting two, show that the
vision of the artist is as clear and his touch as firm as ever. "*Le
Voyageur*" and the "*Postillon revenant haut le pied,*" both executed
since 1883, are replete with the fine qualities of this artist's better
work; and, in the belief of the writer, the former must ever rank as
one of his greatest productions.

Aimé Morot is an emphatic expressionist. In telling his stories he
leaves no doubt as to his real intentions. His enormous canvas
"*Reichoffen,*" which depicts the famous charge of MacMahon's
Eighth and Ninth Cuirassiers, is the largest in the Exhibition, and
is a work of undoubted merit. It has the grand rush, which nearly
all the pictures of charging cavalry lack. Although the horses in
the front rank of the charging column may be flying through the
air instead of running at full speed upon the earth, the great effect to
be sought for is there. The go, the rattle, the clang of war, are on the
canvas as, perhaps, they have never been on any other. "*Le bon
Samaritain,*" is a work quite opposite in character. In this nothing
is done for effect, but a plain story is simply and truthfully told.
The Samaritan, his donkey, and his suffering charge, form one of
the most completely satisfactory and finely executed groups in the
Exhibition. The two human figures will bear the closest critical
scrutiny. The drawing betrays an unusual knowledge of the human
anatomy.

Puvis de Chavannes, one of the most imaginative of the later
French painters, does not exhibit. but reference is made in the catalogue to several of his well-known works, his grand decorative composition, "*Pro Patriâ ludus,*" now in the Amiens Museum, heading
the list.

Of J. François Raffaellé who has a persistent set of outspoken ad-
mirers, it may be safely said, that he has the faculty of seeing clearly
and describing sharply, so as to leave no doubt as to his intentions.
But there is a great difference of opinion as to his general scheme of
color. Doubtless in many instances his coloring is forced and unnatural ; he is nevertheless a master of strong expression, and shows
originality and facility in drawing.

Alfred Roll is one of the most thoroughly distinctive of the younger
French artists. His ten works exhibited display a very wide range
of accomplishment, and establish conclusively his right to a position
among the foremost painters of his time. His "*La fête de Silène*"
is very typical of his strongly expressive work. It shows a jovial
old Silenus mounted on his ass, surrounded by attendant nymphs,

and in his very best mood. "*La grève des Mineurs*," and "*Le Travail—Chantier de Suresnes*," are strikingly realistic. The scenes are depicted with great directness and strength of purpose, but it is doubtful if the subjects are worthy of the valuable labor bestowed upon them. Three others, "*Femme et Taureau*," "*En Normandie*," and "*Manda Lamétrie, fermière*," are pastoral poems on canvas. They are all pitched in the same charming key of tender color, and are specially attractive by their fanciful, and at the same time truthful, expression of the simplest realities.

Joseph Wencker, together with his seven portraits, displays two important compositions of another kind. The larger of the two, "*Prédication de St. Jean Chrysostem contre l'Impératrice Eudoxie*," is spirited and picturesquely composed. It is an historical work of more than ordinary interest. It tells its story so plainly that the dullest may understand it.

From Cormon, Delacroix, Faivre, Jamin, and Nemoz, we have a group of works representing imaginary scenes appertaining to the everyday life of the stone age. These show great originality, are skillfully executed, and are sure to interest all who are in search of the extremely curious.

Among other living French artists exhibiting interesting works—very skillfully treated in many instances—may be mentioned the names of Barrias, Bloch, Bordes, Boutigny, Bramtot, Brouillet, Carrière, Chartran, Chigot, Clairin, Dawant, Delahaye, Dubois, Ferrier, Friant, Geoffroy, Giacomotti, Gilbert, Giradot, Humbert, Jean-Nicot, Krug, Lagarde, Le Blant, Lefebvre, Le Poittevin, Lesur, Maillard, Merson, Montenard, Moreau de Tours, Perrandau, Perret, Rochegrosse, Roy, Saintpierre, Tissot, and Weerts.

WATER COLORS AND PASTELS.

The collection of two hundred and fourteen water colors, pastels, miniatures, and various drawings in the competitive part of the French section, is not remarkable for artistic work. There are very few pieces worthy of special notice. Standing out conspicuously among these are the six pastels by J. Charles Cazin. They show his usual facility for original composition, and much delicacy of touch. Among others of exceptional merit may be mentioned those of Bida, Doucet, and Renouard, and after these Allonge, Bayard, Gagnairt, Carrier, Belleuse, Eliot, Mme. Guyon, Iwill, Mlle. Pompey. Raffaelli, and Rivoire.

SCULPTURE.

From the time of Donatello—the point of departure from the stiff and unnatural Gothic sculpture—no modern nation has possessed at any period of its history a more remarkable group of great sculptors than is to be found in France at this time. Much of their stat-mary displays the grace of pose, the beauty of outline, and vigor of execution that we find in the works of the great Greek masters. For boldness and originality of conception, some of their statues stand unrivaled in our later times. These sculptors are not the outgrowth of any school or system of teaching, for their works bear no flavor of the academy. They are individual and independent, and in the simplicity and directness of their conceptions we see the achievement of masters. Very noticeable, too, in their work, is the absence of any attempt at trifling with nature, so as to produce cheap effects which please the vulgar eye. Such qualities denote the true greatness that comes from earnestness. The writer regrets that he can do no more than briefly notice in this report a few of the more prominent among the French sculptors whose works were to be found at the Exhibition.

M. L. E. Albert Lefevrre contributes six pieces. This artist has the faculty of expressing sentiment, but is often uncertain in his execution. His statue of *"Adolescence"* is that of a young girl standing in a simple pose, her arms raised to her head, and looking dreamily into the future. It is beautifully modeled, is exquisite in sentiment, and gracefully posed. Several of the sculptor's other works are interesting, but they can not be compared to this one.

Paul Aubé's statue of Bailly is perhaps the best costumed figure in the Exhibition. It is that of a man standing simply and firmly, holding in his left hand the formula of the famous oath of the *"Jeu de paume,"* while his right hand is raised. The gesture is solemn, and the entire figure is full of dignity. Other works of this sculptor are marked by the same simplicity and strength.

Alfred Boucher is the artist of a notable group, " *Au but,*" a foot race. Three naked runners are nearing the goal with outstretched hands, every line of the faces expressing anxiety, and the figures the utmost physical exertion. This group represents a great effort, and is as far from the conventional as possible. There is, however, sameness of expression and action in the figures, but the idea of movement is conveyed with singular vigor.

Auguste Cain appears to be as nearly the successor of Barye, as we can expect any sculptor to be. He is dramatic in sentiment and movement, but he does not attain to the combined simplicity and vigor so admirable in Barye's works. He never seems to perfectly understand the character of the animal he represents. His " *Rhinocéros attaqué par des tigres,*" and his " *Lion terrassant un crocodile,*" both bronze groups, are imposing and interesting; and were it not for the recollection of the artist's great predecessor, they might be regarded as triumphs of sculpture in relation to the brute creation.

Jules Dalou exhibits two very large high reliefs and several busts. All are strong, bold in execution, and indicate extensive knowledge

as well as talent. His great masterpiece illustrates a famous scene at
the commencement of the French Revolution at a meeting of the
États Généraux. The King, after delivering his speech, left the hall,
followed by the nobles and part of the clergy. The other deputies
were ordered to leave. The Marquis de Brèze, master of ceremonies,
entering, asked Bailly, the president, if he had heard the King's
command, and received the never-to be-forgotten answer from Mirabeau, "Go and tell your master we are here by the power of the
people, and will only be dismissed by the power of bayonets." The
work is worthy the great and patriotic event it represents. The
illusion as to depth, and great masses of men is perfect, and there
is wonderful variety in expression and attitude. Some are calmly
taking in the situation, others, more or less excited, are talking among
themselves. The work is as natural as it is energetic. In the whole
composition there is but one exaggeration; the figure of Mirabeau
is somewhat theatrical, rather than dramatic. Nevertheless the
story is forcibly told; and we have here one of the finest high reliefs
in existence, and possibly the greatest ever modeled by the hand of
man.

Paul Dubois is the accomplished director of the *École des Beaux
Arts.* In addition to his reputation for scholarship in connection
with the fine arts, he is regarded as a fine portrait painter and a
good sculptor. He is influenced by the Italian Renaissance, has no
great originality, but he sees the details of nature and executes his
works in a spirit of refinement. He has contributed to the Exhibition four sitting statues to be placed at the angles of the monument
to General Lamoricière in the Cathedral at Nantes. These are "*La
Charité,*" a woman with two infants on her knees, charming in sentiment and composition; "*La Foi,*" a young girl, with hands clasped
and face raised in prayer, very expressive of religious fervor; *Le
courage militaire,*" and "*L' Etude.*" The two last, like the others,
are carefully executed with due reference to correct expression.
Little bits of drapery and other details minutely worked do not,
however, suggest grandeur or strength. The artist's other statues,
"*Le Chanteur Florentin,*" and "*Eve naissante,*" are more in the
style wherein this sculptor is seen at his best.

Léon Fagel has scored a success with his statue of Chevreul, the
centenarian scientist, dressed in the unpicturesque costume of to-
day. The head is very lifelike, and the whole composition is easy
and natural. The sculptor's five other contributions show skill but
not greatness.

It has been said of J. A. J. Falguière that he is a sculptor of fine
artistic instinct, but that the enthusiasm of his southern nature
causes him to be indifferent to certain aspects of his work, and very
unequal. He does what pleases him, without caring whether it
pleases others or not. His "*Un vainqueur au combat de Coqs*" is a

GORILLA AND WOMAN, BY FREMIET.

THE NYMPH ECHO, BY GAUDEZ.

young boy holding with his right arm a victorious game-cock, and snapping his fingers with delight. It is a little masterpiece, beautifully modeled, and finely expressive of the high spirits of youth. The other piece exhibited, " *Tarcisius, Martyr Chrétien,*" is a figure of a young martyr who has been stoned to death, and who is pressing to his breast the Christian emblem. The work is very touching in sentiment.

Emmanuel Fremiet is one of the greatest of living French sculptors. His individuality is strongly impressed upon his work; every piece may be said to bear the sign manual of the man. His terribly repulsive but wonderfully vigorous group of a gorilla carrying off a struggling woman limp and half crushed in its powerful grasp, and holding a stone in one hand to throw at the pursuer, is a marvel of exciting realism. No description can give the least conception of the strength of this composition. The contrast that it presents of physical weakness and power is admirable. In every line the beast is the brute of brutes. The whole presents a terrible vision and, possibly, not much of an exaggeration of the lowest side of human nature. It shows the masterly touch in the manipulation of masses and details, and is most artistically composed. This group is a partial repetition of one that figured in the Exhibition of 1860. In that the gorilla was seen dragging his victim instead of carrying her. It was considered so shocking by the Salon Jury that they refused it, but the Minister of Fine Arts gave it a separate room at the Exhibition of that year. Another of his famous groups now exhibiting, " *Le Denicheur d'Ourrons,*" represents the struggle of an old hunter with a she bear that has caught him in the act of carrying off her young. The contest is to the death, the knife is doing its fatal work, and so are the strong arms of the enraged mother. This composition is fierce and full of agony. In another striking group by Fremiet, " *L'Ours et l'homme à l'age de Pierre,*" we see an almost naked savage holding in his hands the head of a bear that he has just overcome, and wildly dancing in the excitement of his triumph. Although this is purely a work of the imagination, it seems to revive an epoch in the unrecorded history of man. There is an intense movement in the works of this artist, which renders them even more lifelike than those of Barye. He is the sculptor of all living forms, and his works are unparalleled for intensity of movement. The sculptural construction, the bones, the extremes of natural action, are perfectly understood and rendered. All of his work is carried to the highest point of comprehensiveness; when it is delicate it surpasses nature, when beastly most brutal, yet not vulgar, and when vigorous nothing can be more so. He is one of the few artists of these days who have produced thoroughly good equestrian statues, which can be compared to the best of the Italian Renaissance.

Adrien Gaudez contributes two statues, " *La nymphe Echo,*" and

"*Parmentier:*" both are strong works, but the former is the most beautiful female statue in the Exhibition. The girlish but well developed form exquisitely feminine and full of simple grace. It is a genuine work of art, free from all affectation. In all the productions of this talented artist are to be observed a fine appreciation of simplicity and an honest purpose to aim only at natural effects.

Claude G. B. E. Guillaume is a learned academician who produces work of an absolutely peculiar kind, which pleases the multitude. The most representative among his ten exhibits is the "*Mariage Romain,*" a group of two figures in marble. It is formal to an extreme degree, and stands more for art than nature, and may be regarded as an inoffensive example of purely academic work.

Antonin Mercie is represented by five pieces. His work generally is very pleasing. "*Le Souvenir*" (a figure for a tomb) is in many respects charming, but lacks the grandeur and spirit that would stamp it as the work of a great artist. His "*Quand Même,*" a woman in modern Alsatian costume, taking the gun from the hands of a dying soldier to defend her country, is marked by a fine spirit, but the general effect is greatly marred by superabundance of detail.

The five works of that wonderful artist, Auguste Rodin, stamp him as one of the greatest sculptors of modern times. He unlocks the secrets hidden in the human form, and applies them to the noblest and grandest uses of art. He also knows the human mind, and is a master of its most subtle expressions and manifestations. It may be said of him that he never busies himself about trifles. His work is always suggestive of more than is seen, and compels serious consideration. Where the Greeks excelled he also excels, and among moderns the greatest of them all, Michael Angelo alone, has surpassed him in the originality of his conceptions. While he understands the Greeks so well he is no imitator of them. He sees nature with his own eyes and works out his impressions in his own way. The secret of Rodin's success may be explained by the high development in him of the art instinct, his extensive knowlege of the literature of art, his disregard of commercial considerations, his fixed determination to avoid littleness in execution, and to accomplish his results by the simplest means. Of the five works he exhibits, "*L'Age d'airain*" is the most complete embodiment of his style. It is a nude figure of a young man, his arms uplifted, one hand pressing his head, the other clenched, expressing pain. No words can describe the beauty of its simple lines, or the intensity of the expression portrayed. It is so strong, delicate, and natural in its construction that there seems to be nothing omitted save the power to move. This work, however, was not a success in the Salon of 1877, and, but for a few discriminating artists who admired it, it would have been refused. It was accepted, but was placed in an out-of-the-way corner, and the sculptor was accused of having *cast it from*

THE ARYAN AGE, BY RODIN.

nature. Twelve years have passed since then, and now, in the great Exhibition of the World's Art, it is admitted to be one of the astonishing masterpieces of modern times. In 1884, another fine work by Rodin was refused at the salon, and he was accused of having cast it from some old Greek statue. His later busts of Hugo, Dalou, and Proust are true works of art; better than mere portraits, they reveal something of the inner character of the men they represent, and, like his other productions, show masterly handling. His finest work, and surely the most grandly and solemnly impressive of our later times, is his group of "*Bourgeois de Calais.*" It illustrates an historical incident; that of the leading citizens of Calais appearing before the English conqueror in answer to his summons, with ropes round their necks, in order to save the town from pillage and destruction. This is a truly noble work, lofty in conception, and most impressively treated.

Réné de Saint-Marceaux contributes four interesting pieces. "*L'Arlequin*" is a small statue excellent in pose, skillfully finished, and very expressive of gay and mischievous humor.

Of the works of Jean Turcan, "*L'Areugle et le Paralytique,*" a marble group, is the most important. It represents a blind man, directed in his path by a paralytic whom he is carrying on his back. Without being a work of genius, this may be regarded as very good sculpture. It is unconventional, and has other virtues; the torso of the blind man, for instance, is beautifully modeled, and the whole composition is interesting by its novelty and evident sincerity of purpose.

Among sculptors who appear in the French section, but are not mentioned in the foregoing remarks, are many whose work in other countries would be rightly regarded as far superior to that of those mechanical mud-pilers who have fashioned most of the commemorative statuary that is supposed to adorn modern cities of the world.

ENGRAVINGS.

It would be beyond the intent and scope of this report to attempt anything like a just and comprehensive notice of the excellent work to be found among the four hundred and forty-four productions by French engravers, exhibited under the head of "*Gravures et Lithographies.*" The collection is as interesting and artistic of its kind as any other in the exhibition. It moreover makes us realize that the greatest engravers of to-day are equal to the best of those in the past. Among the finest examples shown may be mentioned a portrait, after Van Dyck, by Charles Baude; the "*Parting Day,*" after Leader, by Brunet Debaines; the "*Chocolate Girl,*" after Liotard, by F. Eugène Burney; the "*Minuet,*" after Jacquet, by F. Eugène Champollion; the "*Storm,*" after Diaz, by Theophile Chaurel; Darwin, after John Collier, by Léopold Flameng; nine wood engravings, after drawings by Rochegrosse, Raffaelli, Renouard, and Richemond, by Mlle. Marie Genty; the *"Drawing Master,"* after Meissonier, by Achille Jacquet; the *" Gunsmith,"* after Fortuny, by C. Louis Kratké; *" Miss Fanny and Dog,"* after Seymour, by Adolphe Lalauze; the *"Meeting of the States General, June 23, 1789,"* after Dalou, by Alphonse Lamotte; three wood engravings of scenes around Paris, after drawings by the engraver, Louis A. Lepère; the *"Man at the Window,"* after Meissonier, by Paul E. LeRat; a bust of Dalou, after Rodin, by H. Auguste Leveille; the *"Souvenir,"* after Chaplin, by Stephane Pannemacker. Charles A. Waltner is represented by many fine examples of his work, and there are contributions by other artists of merit.

FRENCH COLONIES.

A small number of exhibits from Algeria and other French colonies brings us to the close of the competitive part of the French section. These colonial works do not appear to be of sufficient importance to call for special mention. The art sections of other nations will now be considered in the order in which they occur in the official catalogue.

GERMANY.

That country was not represented by many works of its best men, but artists of German nationality residing in various parts of Europe, contribute one hundred and one exhibits to the Exhibition. Among these were to be found several which in conception, scheme of color and general treatment, stand quite by themselves. They are toned after the manner of some of the strong colorists of the Venetian and Dutch schools, figures and faces being carefully painted so as to express national, rather than personal, characteristics.

GERMAN PAINTERS.

Albert Keller, of Munich, has a fairly good and interesting portrait of a lady, and also a study of the nude. Gotthardt Keuhl, who lives in Paris, has six works, all interiors, neither French nor German in treatment. They are *legers* as to color, subject, and composition, but are not offensive, and are calculated to please the majority of fairly cultivated people, who believe they admire the arts and like pictures of a story-telling order.

Wilhelm Leibl, of Rosenheim, Bavaria, contributes six works. Three of them, *"Femmes de Dachau," "Vieux Paysan et jeune fille,"* and *"Paysanne de Vorarlberg et enfant,"* are notable for the qualities mentioned at the head of this notice. They are strong character works, and the subjects of them could never be mistaken for other than Bavarian peasants. The face of the old man in the second work named is quite repulsive, but is undoubtedly an extremely truthful portrait of a low type of Bavarian slave of the shovel. The face of the young girl is expressive of innocence and characteristic of a nationality.

Max Liebermann, of Berlin, exhibits six works, all fairly good, and thoroughly representative of himself. The "*Cour de la Maison des Invalides à Amsterdam*" and "*Cour de la Maison des Orphelines à Amsterdam*" are the most important. In each the figures are numerous, carefully painted, and naturally grouped, the whole presenting truthfully everyday scenes, without any attempt at the picturesque. The works of this artist are highly esteemed in Germany.

Charles Meyer, of Munich, has three interesting pictures, which, however, are not so well painted as they are composed. "*Le fumeur*," a man in an old costume smoking, is conventional. The deep, warm tone shows the influence of bygone colorists upon the artist. "*Le conte mystérieux*" is a group of old men sitting round a table, eagerly listening to the thrilling story of one of the party. The picture is well composed, and were it not for some defects of color it would be an interesting work.

Hansolde, of Teekamp, Schleswig-Holstein, has sent two paintings, "*Allant à l'Eglise*" and "*Le Matin*," both creditable, and the former particularly interesting.

Friedrich Karl von Uhde, of Munich, has contributed two works, his "*Last Supper*" ("*La Cène*") being regarded as one of considerable importance. Perhaps the reputation of the artist has had something to do with this. To the writer, however, the work seems crude, and painted with little regard to supposed facts and probabilities. The entire group is composed of men whose types might be found on the wharf of any city of northern Europe. There is not a face among them that bears the least indication of Semitic origin, nor do their expressions and gestures betray those qualities of mind which are reasonably attributed to the nearest friends and disciples of Christ. The composition is without dignity, and fails totally to give an adequate idea of the solemnity of the great scene which it is supposed to represent. "*La petite Emilie*" is a simpler but better work. The subject is a young peasant girl coming through a rough stubble field, painted in the realistic manner of to-day. It is a matter-of-fact peasant portrait that answers the aim of the realist, but suggests nothing.

ETCHINGS.

Karl Koepping is represented by two etchings, *Les Syndics des Drapiers*" and the portrait of an old man. Both are after works by Rembrandt, and the technical skill shown in them reflects the utmost credit upon the artist. The writer can conceive of nothing finer and broader in the way of etchings than these reproductions of works by the greatest Dutch master. They must be reckoned among the most remarkable examples in existence of the art of drawing upon copper with *aqua fortis*.

The majority of the works in the German section do not rise above mediocrity. It is not difficult to perceive that in them the commercial aim predominates.

AUSTRIA-HUNGARY.

Austria and Hungary are represented in all classes of the art section by one hundred and fifty-nine exhibits. Probably, for the reason that Austria is one of the non-recognizing governments, the collection does not show forth in a comprehensive sense the present condition of art in that country. It nevertheless contains several artistic and notable works quite worthy of special mention.

AUSTRIAN AND HUNGARIAN PAINTERS.

Vacslav Brozik has five paintings, one of which, "*La défenestration de Prague*," is a very large and ambitious composition. The historical event that it is intended to depict was an act of violence that led to the Thirty Years' War. The imperial councilors, together with their secretary, are being thrown out of a window, because of their refusal to subscribe to the demands of the justly enraged Protestants headed by the Count of Thurn. One of the councilors, the central figure, is struggling with those who have seized him, and his movements, and the expression of his face, betray such abject cowardice as to destroy the entire dignity of the composition, and to render it ridiculous. Much better than this is the artist's unpretentious canvas, "*Le Retour des Champs*," which, as a cattle piece, is at least inoffensive. His other three works are of no particular interest.

Blaise Bukovac exhibits six paintings, not one of which is of great value. "*Le printemps de la vie*" is, however, a pleasing composition, expressive of the subject, and delicate in color.

Edouard Charlemont is represented by thirteen works. Three are portraits, not above the average. "*Les Pages*" is a large, carefully painted canvas, showing a very earnest attempt to accomplish something of value; but the complete want of texture and the color hardness have rendered the attempt futile. The nine others are small figure pieces, hard, unsympathetic, and as regards execution, false in every essential.

Adolphe Hirschel, in one of his two exhibits, gives a glimpse of of the past at Rome in the year 590. This work is not an entire success, but it contains bits of careful painting of old marbles, which render it of great interest to those who admire elaborate and painstaking art.

Albert Hynais in five of his works displays considerable facility for purely decorative composition. His figures are often graceful, the arrangement of his groups effective, and the high light tones of color are just what is required for decorative purposes. His two portraits are without interest.

Jan Matejko has covered an enormous canvas with a great deal of paint. It is among the largest of the exhibition, and is entitled "*Kosciusko après la bataille de Raclavice.*" It is a most diffuse composition, conceived without definite ideas as to centralization of effect, spotty in color, and does not realize the grandeur of a great historical scene.

Michel de Munkacsy has a world-wide reputation, and is regarded by many persons as one of the great artists of the day. His "*Christ before Pilate*" and his "*Christ at Calvary,*" which reappear at this Exhibition, are so well known that no description of them is necessary here. They are most ambitious works, and must have cost the artist a world of thought and labor. They are serious, large in execution, and are earnest efforts in a great direction. In the opinion of the writer they are in every respect the best achievements of this artist.

Jules de Prayer is represented by three large works, depicting scenes connected with the sad fate of Sir John Franklin and his companions in the Arctic regions. They suggest the solemnity of that awful history more vividly than has ever been done before.

Rudolph Ribarz is an artist who is generally correct in his outdoor effects. He is a close follower of nature, throws his individuality into what he does, and has the rare faculty of making an interesting picture from an uninteresting subject. Of his ten contributions the one entitled, "*Overschie ; Holland,*"—a marine piece, with boats, and buildings on the shore. is the most important.

Vacslav Sochor is represented by two works: "*Procession de la Fête-Dieu en Bohème,*" and a portrait. In the former, a gaudy, commonplace scene of a Catholic country, is treated in a conventional spirit. It is glaringly offensive in color, and is altogether inferior to the better theatrical scene painting. Unfortunately its enormous size brings it prominently into notice.

Othon de Thoren, a well-known painter of cattle pieces, a member of the International Jury, died within three days after the work of judging was completed. His seven contributions are thoroughly representative of his life's work. Several are exceedingly tender in color, and show a good understanding of perspective, and the picturesque in composition. While the works of this artist may not be regarded as great, they are much nearer the truth, and more pleasing than those of many others who have greater reputations.

BELGIUM.

The Kingdom of Belgium is represented by four hundred and fifty exhibits, of which two hundred and fifty-two are oil paintings. Among the latter are several of marked merit, and the collection, taken as a whole, reflects great credit upon the Belgian artists. The influence of contemporary French art upon them is easily recognizable, but only in few instances, so far as this collection is concerned, can it be said to have been detrimental to them. The truth is, that the stronger among the Belgian artists possess the necessary power and the faculty of asserting themselves.

BELGIAN PAINTERS.

Emile Claus has three charming landscapes, very characteristic of his manner. They are true to nature, and are marked by much tender sentiment. The "*Passage d'Eau*," a daintily painted piece, is the most highly elaborated of the three, and is such a work as an admirer of the simple and beautiful must perforce appreciate.

Franz Courtens, who, in the belief of the writer, is one of the greatest living landscape artists, is represented by five works. The strong points with him are his deep feeling for nature, his intimate familiarity with its best pictorial phases, and a fine instinct that enables him to apply them to higher purposes of art. His knowledge of technical resources enables him to derive the fullest value from his rare power of selection. Although he never has recourse to slap-dash to produce his effects, which bear the stamp of careful, solid, and honest work, they are boldly and broadly conveyed. His perspective is just, the horizon line is placed where it belongs in nature, and when a bit of architecture or shipping is introduced, the drawing and texture are faultless. His most important work among those now exhibited is "*Le retour de l'office*," but the most charming are "*La pluie d'or*" and "*Le barque à Moules*." Together they give a good idea of the better qualities of that artist.

Emile Delpérée has sent a most ambitious picture; "*Martin Luther à la Diète de Worms.*" It is an earnest attempt to adequately commemorate one of the most important events in the history of civilization, but it is only a partial success. It is somewhat theatrical rather than dramatic as the artist intended.

Jean Pierre Lamorinière has three works of considerable merit. They of marked individuality, and are worthy of the artist, who is greatly esteemed in his own country; but to the writer they appear to be only careful studies of trees and topography for studio use.

Robert Mols displays a very long canvas entitled "*Rade d'Anvers.*" It is in fact the water front of Antwerp. It has the merit of veracity, and is strictly panoramic.

Alfred Stevens is perhaps better known out of Belgium than any other Belgian artist. He contributes to this Exhibition seventeen pictures. They show great fertility of resource, facility for rapid production, and leave upon the beholder an impression that there are plenty more of the same sort where those came from.

Alexandre Struys has sent only two works, but each bears the signs by which we know a man of sentiment and an earnest artist. "*Le gagne pain*" is a scene of everyday life—an interior with a peasant mother giving medicine to a son who is ill. It is a very simple story wonderfully told. The other, entitled "*Mort*," is sternly pathetic. A dead man is lying in his coffin and a woman is upon her knees. This is the whole subject, but it is thrillingly interpreted. The artist possesses singular power in dealing with human emotions.

Jan van Beers exhibits his painting of the yacht, the rowboat, the waiting crew, and the conventional yachtsman, handing down the stairs, presumably into the boat, the young lady in correct attire. Besides this he shows thirteen other trifles, all in his usual style, save one little landscape belonging to the Comtesse de Flandre, which is charming, being simple in subject and truly artistic in execution.

Jan Verhas is represented by four important works of strong individuality. They could never be mistaken for those of another man. One that stands out prominently is "*La révue des écoles*"—the children of Brussels passing in front of the King. This is a masterly character-work that brings Belgium generally before the spectator, and Brussels in particular. The whole scene is as natural as possible. The first rank of children—beautiful little girls—are not French, German, or Dutch, but distinctly Belgians, and so it is with the rest. The type is clearly set forth. The atmosphere, the sky, the town are there, and the exact perspective renders the architectural effect perfect. The writer once heard an artist call this a mechanical picture. Its mechanics are such as the majority of artists would do well to master. The other three works are not large, but they are perfectly representative.

Theodore Verstraete is another of the good Belgian landscape painters. He exhibits four pieces. "*Le lever de lune à la Bruyère*," contains in the foreground some charming work, but fails in aërial perspective. "*Soirée de Novembre*" seems more satisfactory, and reminds one a little of the better landscapes of Millet.

Alfred Verwee is an artist of considerable individuality, and he has sent four works. He paints cattle pictures, but by no means of the sort to which we are most accustomed. His art is virile. His productions are not always true to nature, but he never trifles. In some of his paintings he shows peculiar aptitude for conveying an idea of the grandeur of great space.

Emile Wauters, another of the esteemed Belgian painters is represented by twelve works, nine of which are portraits. "*Cosme*

Somzée" a boy on horseback with a dog holding a whip, is a large ambitious composition, and so is another portrait. that of the boy's mother. Both rise far above mediocrity in portraiture. To the writer, however. the artist's Eastern scenes appear to be his most successful works. Their composition and *technique* are good, and they have the local color of Egyptain life.

There are other Belgian artists who are not considered to be in the first rank, but several of whom produce acceptable works; among these last may be named Artan, Asselberghs. Mlle. Beernaert, Bouvir, Broerman, Mme. Collart, D'Anethan, Dedans, De la Hoese, Den Duyts, De Smeth, Mlle. De Vign, Dierick, Ronner, (Alice), Simons, Smits. Stallaert, Stobbaerts, Zytgadt, Van Biesbroeck, Vanderecht, Van Havermaet, Van Hove, Verhaert, and Vanhayden.

BELGIAN SCULPTORS.

After the French the Belgian sculpture is the best in the Exhibition. The strongest men have originality, and much of their better work shows that they are influenced by the study of the Gothic. In the productions of others we find a reflection of the commonplace and handskill of the poorer French workmen.

Guillaume Charlier has three works, all refined in sentiment and forcible in execution. His large composition " *La Justice inspirée par le Droit et la Clémence*," is impressive but rather sketchy. His kneeling statue of a young girl, " *Figure tombale*," is charming in sentiment and pose. His busts are also interesting.

Paul de Vigne is a powerful sculptor in expression, dignity, and strength. His monumental group "*Breidel et De Coninc*" erected in Bruges to the glory of the victors of the battle of Courtrai, fought in 1302, is large and grand in composition and execution; worthy of the great event it commemorates. The three busts by this artist are wonderfully fine. They are studies for heads of figures in his large monuments. For simplicity of handling and expression they are without rivals in the whole Exposition.

Constantin Meunier tells in marble and bronze sad stories of the everyday life of the lowly. " *Le Grison* " is an episode of coal-mining. A mother finds her son among the dead, after an explosion; and the pain expressed in her face as she gazes at the corpse is human, natural, and peculiarly touching. The composition is simple, something after the manner of the early Italians. By the originality of the artist a great effect is produced in combination with perfect repose. There is no trace of exaggerated physical action. Here we have proof of ability of a high order. This sculptor's " *Puddleur* " is of the same kind of art, and tells in awful lines the terrible tale of degradation in the mines. What an expression of low brutality it conveys. In treatment it is like the other; simple, direct and true. These works are surely the outcome of humane impulses in an artist who feels what he does, and it is not his fault if they do not teach a great lesson to the wealthy and thoughtless.

Pierre Charles Vanderstoppen's work conveys the idea of personality, but is somewhat pretentious. "*L'homme a l'epée,*" a young man holding a sword, is a good figure, but a little stiff in pose. "*Le taciturne,*" an old Flemish nobleman, has a character of its own, and conveys to the beholder an idea of nobility. It is certainly one of the good statues of the Exhibition. His "*Saint Michel*" is a man in armor; simple in composition, decorative, and quite mediæval in effect. His other works are fine, but artistically inferior to those mentioned.

There are some good pieces by Braecke, Mignon, and Namur, but not to be compared with the work of those sculptors whose exhibits have been described.

DENMARK.

Of the two hundred and forty-eight works contributed by Denmark one hundred and ninety are oil paintings: and this is about all that can be said of them. To call the majority of these "works of art" would be to make a very reckless use of a term that has been already sufficiently abused. As a rule, they are unsymmetrical, unimaginative, unsentimental, and commonplace as regards subject and composition, while in technical qualities they are rough and uncouth. There are not twenty among them which show that the artist who painted them possessed a sense of the beautiful. Possibly the works of these Danish painters prove that they possess qualities which, among certain artists and writers, pass for boldness, breadth, and strong brush-work. But the presence of all of these virtues combined in a painter does not compensate for the absence of the picturesque.

DANISH PAINTERS.

Michael Ancher, a painter of unaccountable inequality, exhibits eight works. His "*Se tirera-t-il d'affaire?*" a group of fishermen looking out to sea, is a fine composition, well executed, and plainly indicates an artist of talent. His "*Portrait de ma femme*" is also a good work, but his "*Vieillard devant sa maison*" is unworthy of the slightest commendation. The old man is of the very lowest type of humanity, and the whole composition has the qualities of an exceedingly bad chromo. The artist's other paintings are not good, but they are better than this one.

Otto Bache exhibits a portrait rather above the average, and a large picture of two work horses. These are rather well painted, but the work is not artistically composed, nor is it even interesting.

Peter Severin Kroyer, of Copenhagen, contributes seven works, among which is the best in the whole Danish collection. This is "*Le Comité de l'Exposition Française à Copenhagen en* 1888." It

is a large interior filled with portraits of Frenchmen, principally
the more elderly and better known among living artists. It is well
conceived, the portraits are done with a free hand, the postures are
natural, and the grouping is well arranged. It is, beyond all cavil,
a very successful work, and of a kind very difficult to treat successfully. This artist also exhibits a portrait of the director of the
Academy of Fine Arts at Copenhagen, which is dignified and possesses character. His other works on view are not remarkable for
artistic qualities.

L. Tuxen contributes five canvases. Among them is a good portrait of Mme. O. Jacobsen, very simple and direct in treatment. A
remarkable specimen of realism is his " *Italienne sortant du bain.*"
It can not be described, but must be seen to be appreciated. His
other exhibits are not very noteworthy.

Among other artists whose works are fairly good may be mentioned Mme. Ancher, Brendekilde, Hammershöj, Henningsen, Jon-
dorff, Johansen, Mols, Niss, Paulsen, N. K. Skovgaard, Therkildsen,
Wegmann, and Zahrtmann. The drawings in black and white by
Hans Tegner are original, full of character, and very picturesquely
composed.

SPAIN.

The artists of Spain are represented by one hundred and seventy-
nine pieces, one hundred and sixteen of which are oil paintings. This
collection contains more large canvases in proportion to ‖its numbers than any other in the Exhibition. Its appearance is consequently somewhat imposing, but in the matter of artistic worth it
can not be compared to the Spanish collection in the Exhibition of
1878. The present section suffers from the absence of Zamacois'
works, and the charming pictures by the gifted and lamented Fortuny. Nor can anything be found in it equal to the "*Jean de la
Folle*," by Pradilla. It is in vain that one looks for good works to
supply the place of other fine productions that can be called to mind;
moreover, the fact must be recorded that several of the artists whose
work we admired eleven years ago do not appear to advantage now.

SPANISH PAINTERS.

Luis Alvarez, the painter of romantic pictures displaying gaily
dressed men and women, brilliant stuffs and furniture wonderfully
elaborated, has left his old paths and given his attention to subjects
of a more serious character. He has sent to this Exhibition a very
large canvas, "*La chaise de Philippe II; Escurial,* 1597." This
work represents one of the most horrible characters known in history, sitting upon a seat hewn out of the solid rock, to which he has
just been carried. He is pictured in consultation with a minister,
probably over the perpetration of some fresh act of cruelty or injus-

tice. The composition has been intelligently conceived, and seriously and artistically treated.

José J. Aranda contributes five works, among which is a Crucifixion, unrefined in treatment and failing utterly to convey the picture of that appalling event. His " *Les Politiciens* " is conventional, like scores of other works dealing with subjects of the same order. What we see in this, as in others, is an animated but commonplace dispute, that leaves the spectator indifferent. The remaining works are in no way superior to those which have been named.

The late José Casado del Alisal is represented by a marvel of all that is horrible, "*La Cloche de Huesca.*" A middle-aged man with a large, remarkably savage-looking dog, is in a cellar or dungeon, where the wholesale decapitation of human beings has taken place. The floor is strewn with heads, and red with blood. To make the horror still more horrible, there is a blood-dripping head hanging from a rope in the middle of this gruesome subterranean chamber. This terrible scene is wonderfully and faithfully elaborated upon a very large canvas. The work is one of enormous power, but in a fearful direction.

Antonio Gisbert presents another tale of blood, " *Exécution des Torrijos et de leurs compagnons, Malaga, 1831.*" The band of patriots are undergoing military execution. A group of dead bodies is in front of a line of men waiting their turn; others, a second rank, who are to form the next line for execution, are being blindfolded. This is also a large canvas, and the scene is extremely revolting.

Felix Resureccion Hidalgo has sent a canvas of imposing size. "*L'Enfer de Dante,*" very confused and very infernal.

Louis Jimenez has contributed a work of a very different character from those already mentioned. This is " *Une Salle d'hôpital; la visite.*" An emaciated young girl is sitting up in bed, in an ordinary hospital ward, having her lungs examined by a physician. Other physicians and students are standing near awaiting the result. A sad, everyday story is pathetically and humanly told, with sincerity free from affectation. It moves the beholder to sympathize with suffering.

Raimundo de Madrazo has relinquished the painting of ideal subjects and become a painter of portraits of the *beau monde*. They seem to flow from his palette in a continuous stream, but they are hard, cold, unsympathetic, and formal, and convey no idea of the character of those whom they represent. Imagine a large canvas, say, 6 by 4 feet, covered with a deep body of color, in imitation of the dark "Sèvres blue," and upon this the full-length figure of a woman in a dress of the well-known pink of the Sèvres rose teacup, the whole executed as though it were painted upon porcelain and baked, and we have a typical example of the present work of this artist. His figures, however, are all well dressed, and usually appear

as if they belonged to the upper dead-level of society respectability.
In these portraits the effects flowing from a combination of light
and shade are never seen, and a sameness in values pervades the
whole.

José Carbonero Moreno has given us a very large canvas, "*Le duc
de Gandiá devant le cadavre de l'Impératrice Isabelle.*" Here we
have a dead woman in a coffin at one end of the picture, a group of
standing figures at the other end, and the man who is holding the up-
turned lid of the coffin pressing suggestively a handkerchief against
his nose. The whole is well composed and correctly painted, but
the picture excites no interest, and leaves the spectator unmoved
and in doubt as to the purpose.

Francisco Pradilla's large work, "*Reddition de Grenade,*" is an
exceedingly florid military painting, of accomplished *technique*, and
carefully treated generally. It can not be compared, however, to
the great work by which that artist was represented in 1878. It is
overcrowded with figures, which were not necessary to the success
of the composition.

Martin Rico, who is so popular with the dealers and picture buyers of the United States, is now represented by seven works, all bril-
liantly white and sparkingly green. Of course they are said to be
crisp, and possessed of "fine atmospheric effect," but they give us
neither nature nor art.

Emilio Francis y Sala shows a large and forcible composition,
"*Expulsion des Juifs d'Espagne.*" There is considerable skill in
the execution, but it does not tell its story in plain terms. An explanation should have been printed in the catalogue. This artist's
"*Etude de Fruits*" is better than the usual conventional fruit painting.

DRAWINGS.

Armand Jiminez, whose oil paintings have been mentioned, appears to great advantage in his drawings and one water-color. They
are original and strong, and show a refined appreciation of nature.

Daniel Urrabieta Vierge is, in the opinion of the writer, the greatest
Spanish artist living. Certainly, in his peculiar way in the use of pen
and ink, he stands unrivaled. His works prove that he has no sympathy with the empty pretensions, charlatanism, and vices of the
day, and no folly flies without being pierced by his arrow. The great
range of his imagination and his keen perceptions make him a master in the delineation of human passions and weaknesses. Whether
he portrays the vain frump, garbed in a thin wash of austerity on
her way to her devotions, the dishonest beggar with his artificial expression of suppliant misery, the driving of a bargain, the Jew in
pursuit of money, the vanities of the successful grocer's wife, the
supersanctimonious posings of the sleek prelate, or the proud and

overbearing demeanor of the newly made plutocrat, his success in telling his story is always the same. Originality of conception and execution, vitality, force, and vividness of expression, place the works of this artist in the front rank among the best of all times, and it is by no means certain that in his particular line he has ever had his superior.

UNITED STATES.

The exhibits from the United States numbered five hundred and seventy-two, and in quantity came next to the competitive collection of the French, while the fairly good quality of a portion of the work commanded attention and an unexpected amount of appreciation and approval. Several disinterested judges—artists and critics—competent to give intelligent opinions, decided that in merit as well as in magnitude its place was next to the French section. That it did contain a number of well painted, strong, original works is a fact that can not be disputed. It is also true that the collection as a whole was an interesting one, and showed great progress in the several departments of art during the last eleven years.

If we take into consideration the fact that in the French Exhibition of 1878 we had only only one hundred and forty-three oils and water-colors and nineteen engravings, making a total of one hundred and sixty-two, and that in the late Exhibition we had more than three and a half times that number, the relative numerical importance of the two collections becomes clearly apparent. It should, moreover, be borne in mind that what has been accomplished by our artists has been done without the aid of their own Government and with little encouragement from their own people. It is a fact that can not be too much insisted upon that American purchasers who pay large prices, generally buy foreign names, whose pictures may or may not be works of art, and that the meritorious productions of their own countrymen, save when found in the hands of the dealer, they usually pass by unheeded.

It may therefore be taken for granted that whatever credit—and the writer claims that it is considerable—this exhibition of art may reflect upon our country, Americans, as a people, deserve none of it. The credit is due to their leading artists alone, who have toiled, often without reference to commerce, in the truest interest of art, and made the successful uphill fight against a singular combination of unfavorable circumstances, and nearly always without the discriminating support, or even sympathy, of any considerable portion of their countrymen, and no recognition whatever from their Government.

PAINTERS OF THE UNITED STATES.

William S. Allen sent a small canvas of a young girl in gray. The sky and nearly all of the surrounding objects are of the same tone. This work of undoubted merit is entitled "*Le soir, sur le bord du lac.*" It is well composed and delicately painted.

J. Carroll Beckwith exhibits three portraits. The better is the strikingly-lifelike portrait of William Walton. The composition is original, the painting bold and artistic. The others are less successful.

Edward A. Bell contributed a delicate scheme of color, in which he embodies the portrait of a lady. This was his only exhibit, and it is undoubtedly an artistic work.

Henry S. Bisbing was represented by a canvas entitled "*La sieste sur la plage.*" The drawing of the cattle, the details of the landscape, and the treatment of color render this more interesting than most compositions of the same kind; but it is not to be compared to a painting of very exceptional merit exhibited by Mr. Bisbing in the Salon of the present year, 1889.

Robert F. Blum sent his "*Dentillières Vénitiennes,*" a room full of young Venetian women making lace. This is a well-known picture, and is undoubtedly of considerable artistic value. The composition is well conceived, the figures are daintily painted and gracefully posed, and the action generally is good; but there is at one end of the canvas an unfortunate streak of green, and at the other a corresponding one of yellow, and these rather startling blemishes mar the effect of the whole.

Frank M. Boggs contributes three pictures. The most important is the "*Place de la Bastille.*" It belongs to the French Government. In this we have an extreme of what might be termed in art the "French Gray." The sky, the column, the surrounding buildings, the carriages, horses, men, women, and pavements are all gray. But the work is striking, and gives a vivid picture of the scene.

Robert B. Brandegee contributes one among the few fine portraits in the American section. It is simple, quiet, and direct, is free from tinsel effects and undue ornamentation, and is the result of an earnest effort in the right direction.

Frederick A. Bridgman, a well-known painter of Eastern subjects, is represented by six works. The one that commands attention most is "*Le pirate d'Amour,*" a picture in three compartments. In the first we see a young Egyptian girl reading upon a terrace, and just above the parapet the face of a man gazing at her with an expression that corresponds to the title of the picture. In the second compartment the ruffian is struggling with the girl, and in the third she is lying dead in a pool of blood. The second canvas was a puzzle to the French critics; the struggle was not thought by them to explain itself with sufficient clearness. No one, however, need wish the unpleasant story to be told more plainly. It is a spirited and decidedly dramatic picture. "*Fête du Prophète à Oued-el-Kebir,*" and "*Fête Négre à Blida*" are good examples of the work of this painter, but there are better artistic qualities in his "*Marché aux chevaux au Caire*," than in any of those previously mentioned. The horses are remarkably well drawn, and they show their Arabian breed unmistakably. The artist's portrait of "*Madam B.*" is striking, and proves that ho has the power of vividly reproducing the expression of a human face.

Of the three works contributed by Howard Russell Butler, "*Récoltes d'algues marines*" pleases most by its truthfulness. The land and all the details of the coast are very artistically represented.

William M. Chase is a painter of many pictures, embracing a wide range of subjects. Of the eight now exhibited, five are very small landscape studies, and three are portraits. Among these last is one of "*Mrs. G.*," which is in every respect a most commendable work. The full length figure has an easy and natural pose. It is carefully drawn and painted; the general effect is dignified and free from any trick of the trade. One of the other two is unworthy of the artist who painted the one described.

William Anderson Coffin is a close observer, and his four landscapes in this Exhibition proves that he knows the value of the simple forms in which nature abounds. His "*Claire de lune*" is an original and ambitious attempt not altogether unsuccessful, to represent an effect of nature full of technical difficulties.

Kenyon Cox is an earnest seacher after truth, working in many directions, and his four exhibits fairly represent his capabilities. His portrait of Saint-Gaudens, the sculptor, in his studio, is faithful and forcible, and the best of his present exhibits. "*Ombres fuyantes*"—passing shadows—is a curious study of nature, but can not be regarded as a successful or pleasing work of art.

William P. W. Dana is represented by four works, of which the largest and most ambitious is "*Le Christ marchant sur les eaux.*" Of this it can only be written that if its execution had been as correct as its conception was grand, it would be a work of rare dignity and impressiveness. The other three fall much below the merit of a great marine by that artist, called "Solitude," and exhibited in the Exhibition of 1878.

William T. Dannat observes carefully and constructs intelligently. He has qualities which are recognized not only by Americans, but by people of other countries as well. Of his six pictures now exhibited, three represent his most characteristic work. First of all should be mentioned "*Un quatuor*," which will always rank among the masterpieces of American art. It is thoroughly and unmistakably Spanish. If Cervantes or Le Sage had been artists and had painted it, it could not have been more typically and truly Iberian. It is full of life and action, but the effect is obtained without any apparent effort. We feel that the man who is singing is doing so with all the power he possesses, but he is quite at his ease. The young Spanish woman, who is playing the castanets, is throwing all the force and earnestness of her southern nature into the work, but in this expressive physical action there is repose. The same may be said of the mandolin and guitar players in the background. The picture is replete with expression. The drawing of the figures is correct, the costumes are accurately painted, the scheme of color, low in its tones to somberness, is nevertheless rich and harmonious. In a word, the painting is a consummate work of art. The portrait of "*Mlle. H.*" is another sincere painting by this artist. It is only the head of a blond young girl, but it is so simply and truly done that it seems to take us back to the best period of the Dutch school. "*Une sacristie en Aragon*" takes us again to Spain, for it is essentially Spanish. A fat, monumental, well-fed priest sitting erect in his conversation with a Spaniard of the lower order, seated by his side and evidently admiring him. From the expression of the ecclesiastic we feel sure that a very important question has been submitted for his consideration. This work is somewhat satirical. The condition of the priest does not tell the story of long fasts and many fish days. The work is quiet in color, but strong in general treatment. The three remaining paintings by this artist are not in his usual vein, but they show great technical skill.

Charles H. Davis is one of the most distinguished among the present American landscape painters. He has the faculty of selecting simple and beautiful phases of nature, and he paints them in a broad, tender, and unaffected manner. Of his four works now exhibited, "*Une soirée d'hiver*" is the most noteworthy as regards composition and original treatment.

Thomas W. Dewing is one of the better of living American *genre* painters. Unfortunately he is represented by only one work, "*Femme en jaune.*" It is a full length figure of a young woman seated and dressed in yellow. It is an exceptionally artistic little work. The pose is a trifle stiff, and there is an entire absence of anything like sprightly coquetry, which is so telling in a pretty woman. We turn away from this with the satisfaction of having contemplated the "counterfeit presentment" of a perfectly and severely correct specimen of well-bred womanhood.

William L. Dodge has the distinction of having contributed the largest canvas to the American section. It is entitled "*David*," and represents the biblical hero standing over the body of his late gigantic foe. The figure of David is dramatic, and is drawn with considerable power. In the distance there is a shadowy idea of an innumerable host. After contemplating this scene one feels that the story might have been told just as well upon about a quarter of the canvas.

G. Ruger Donoho is represented by two large landscapes. The

one named *"La Marcellerie"* is far the better of the two, and is a very close and carefully painted study from nature.

Henry F. Farny's *"Le danger"* depicts an Indian riding down the slope of a mountain grasping his rifle and evidently on the lookout for an expected foe. The subject is graphically and artistically treated.

Frank Fowler exhibits a portrait under the name of *"Au piano."* It represents a woman on a piano stool, turned away from the instrument. The pose of the figure is easy, and the work has a decided merit both as regards composition and color.

Gilbert Gaul is the only American artist who has devoted his talent to the painting of scenes from our late war. Of the two sent to this Exposition, *"Chargeant la batterie"* is the more interesting. We see a body of infantry charging in the direction of the lights caused by the firing of artillery. The movement of the charging column is free and natural and gives a good idea of the reality. The subject of the other canvas is a wounded officer being held upon his horse, and it gives a fairly true picture of such an incident.

Walter Gay has passed the whole of his artistic career in France, and has justly gained a considerable reputation as a careful painter of *genre* pictures. Within the last three or four years he has changed his style, and now devotes himself to the showy gray and coarsely effective. *"La Charité,"* which is the largest of his six exhibits, is an ultra example of his present work. That it is effective there can be no doubt; but if it is artistic it can only be so at the expense of truth and by a violation of rules which govern the natural relations of the simplest realities. Several of his other works are quieter in color and general execution and approach more nearly the true in art, but their value is not equal to that of his earlier works.

Carl Gutherez is represented by two works. One *"Lux Incarnationis,"* is highly imaginative, and must have cost the artist much thought and labor. It is a daring effort of fancy, and the painter deserves credit for thus straying from the path of the commonplace.

Alexander Harrison stands among the strong artists of his time. He has conquered the ocean and made of it an art field peculiarly his own. No artist represented at the Exhibition has painted the sea more truthfully than he. He prefers the simplest moods of the ocean, the most quiet and measured of wave forms, and transfers his impressions of them directly to canvas. In his pictures there is no attempt to paint the effect of blustering wind and the beating of waves against rocks; he prefers summer quietude and broad, sweeping, easy wave movements. His water tints are as close to nature as paint and brush can make them. *"Crépuscule"* and *"La Vague,"* two of his six works in the Exhibition, are excellent examples of his seascapes. *"En Arcadie"* is a grassy, almost sylvan scene, with nude figures and much sunshine. *"Chateux en Espagne"* is a pic-

ture of a boy stretched at full length at the foot of a sandhill by the
sea. Tired of playing with shells, he is now gazing dreamily into
space. This is undoubtedly one of the artist's better works; the open-
air effect is admirable, and the old story of boyhood's dreams is told
with such simple strength that any one can understand it.

Birge Harrison's "*Novembre*" is the only picture by this artist in
the Exhibition. It is the one that produced such a favorable impression in the Salon several years ago, and was purchased by the
French Government. It is a truthful and charming picture of a
reposeful chestnut wood in late autumn, with the simple figure of a
peasant girl to relieve the solitude. The ground is strewn with red
leaves. The painting is quite free from exaggeration.

Edward L. Henry contributes two works. In his "*Il y a cent
ans*," we have a faithful representation of a southern scene a hundred years ago. The yellow cabriolet, the negro coachman in livery,
the continental costume, and other details, graphically revive the
place and period. This artist deserves credit for trying to keep
alive in the minds of our countrymen some idea of the only picturesque period in our national history.

George Hitchcock works within limited lines, but there is an individuality in what he does. "*La culture des Tulipes*," when exhibited at the Salon, caused a little "sensation" among the critics. It
depicts a Dutch girl walking in a garden of quadrangular tulip beds
of different colors. The subject is a commonplace one, but it has
been so artistically handled that an interesting picture has been
made of it. His other two works now exhibited, "*L'Annonciation*"
and "*Maternité*," are cousins-german to the first named. In each
there is a woman walking among flowers. They are eminently
artistic, and are marked by a rare tone of refinement.

William H. Howe exhibits three landscapes with cattle. Two are
large and very interesting compositions. "*La rentrée des vaches*"
is very broadly treated, and the whole construction of the work shows
careful study and artistic appreciation of the value of picturesque
forms. The cattle are well drawn, and their action natural. " *Le
Repos* " is another and a large work, showing the same qualities as the
one described.

Daniel Ridgway Knight is among the most successful of American
artists of to-day. His work is popular for its pleasing qualities, and
as a rule is picturesque. Some artists assert that he elaborates and
finishes too much, that his peasants are too well dressed and clean of
face, that they savor of the Opera Comique, etc. Their cleanness,
however, if imaginative, is a relieving merit, since they are usually
painted so dirty. If, as is alleged, Mr. Knight does take liberties
with the exact truth, he should be forgiven, for his error is in the
interest of the beautiful—as he sees it.

One of his three works now exhibited, "*L'Appel au passeur*," is eminently representative of his style. Two of his peasant girls are on the bank of the Seine hailing a ferryboat on the opposite side. They are clean, smiling, and pretty, and such girls as any person of taste would be willing to know. The landscape is soft and harmonious in tone. The whole is well composed and worked out with a just observation of natural forms. His other two works set forth his merits or demerits as an artist, but not so strongly as " *L'Appel au passeur.*"

Walter MacEwen has contributed three Dutch scenes of considerable interest. They are all figure pieces and interiors. " *Une histoire de revenant* " shows a much scattered group of women spinning, dressed in red, and covers almost in a line. the whole length of the canvas. This work has many strong points, and if it were not for its faulty composition it would be of great artistic value. The other paintings are likewise of conspicuous merit.

J. Gari Melchers is another of the young American painters possessing originality. In his researches among the Dutch he has found something new, although it is as old as the people themselves. He has observed something in their daily life worth painting that no artist had seen before in the same way. Such discoveries are only made by the close observer and careful student of human nature. " *La Communion,*" the largest of his four canvases, gives the interior of a Protestant church; plain walls, desk, seats, and table, the clergyman in his professional garb in the act of administering the sacrament to the working-class congregation in their carefully preserved clothing of many colors. A feeling of sincere and confiding devotion pervades the whole scene, which is singularly impressive. Were it not for the strange hardness of the flesh tints. which give the faces an almost wooden appearance, this work might be regarded as a complete artistic success. In " *La Prêche,*" another church interior of smaller size, the hard painting of the larger work is to an extent avoided. " *Les pilotes*" an interior with a group of Dutch sailors smoking, has still less of this color hardness. It is typical and full of character, a homely scene truthfully and artistically painted.

H. Humphrey Moore exhibits a considerable number of small studies from the everyday life of the Japanese. Several of these are singularly artistic in treatment, and they have the advantage of being actual scenes drawn on the spot by a careful observer.

Henry Mosler has made himself master of the Brittany peasants' households. He portrays with equal force their joys and sorrows, and many of his works suggest that he must derive a solemn pleasure from depicting the pathetic side of their lives. " *Le retour,*" " *Les derniers sacrements,*" and " *Les derniers moments,*" the first named in the Luxembourg Gallery, and the two last in the present Exhibition, are all pitched in the same key, and in each the interest centers upon a death scene. These works tell their story in such a manner as to excite the sympathy of the beholder.

J. Douglas Patrick is represented by one large canvas, "*Brutalité.*" It is the oft-told tale of the heavy load, the weary, willing horse, the brutal driver armed with a club beating the overworked animal which accident has placed in his power. The picture is a telling one: in looking at it one realizes all the baseness of the too common acts of cruelty towards one of the noblest and most useful of the animal creation.

Charles Sprague Pearce commenced his artistic career by successfully painting scriptural subjects. He afterwards produced some very clever *genre* pictures, and latterly we find him perfectly at home among the peasants and sheep pastures of Picardy. In this Exhibition he is represented by four works, of which "*La bergère*" is the most important. The picture is large and decidedly of the "French grey" order now in vogue, but this particular grey is the property of the artist. The subject is a young peasant girl tending a flock of sheep on the side of a hill. Her attitude and her pensive expression indicate that her thoughts are wandering far away from her flock. Perhaps she is longing for the indefinite brighter days. There is fine sentiment in this genuine bit of rusticity, and in the treatment of outdoor effects the artist has shown great technical skill. This painting has received more official honors than has usually been bestowed upon the better works of American artists. The list is as follows: A third-class medal at the Salon of 1883; a gold medal at Munich 1887, and a special gold medal of honor, the highest awarded at Ghent, in 1888. The three other works exhibited by this painter likewise convey a good idea of his artistic qualities.

Henry G. Plumb contributes the smallest canvas to the American section. It is called "*Les Orphelines,*" and represents the mother mouse caught in the old-fashioned trap, head in wire and body out, while the interesting family of little orphans are trying to solve the mystery of her stillness. The story is so pathetically told that we turn away from the picture hating the inventor of the cruel trap.

Charles Stanley Reinhart is represented among the oil paintings by six canvases. The largest and most ambitious are "*Une épave,*" and "*L'attente des absents.*" The first is a coast scene of a group of fisher people and a *gendarme* assembled near the body of a drowned sailor ; the second is a group of women on the anxious lookout over the sea for absent relatives. Both pictures are spirited and lifelike reproductions of actualities, and prove conclusively that this artist has the faculty of graphically depicting what he sees. His other oil paintings do justice to his capabilities.

William T. Richards, the best known of American marine painters, is represented by one notable canvas. It is a coast scene, artistically treated, but it is not an example of his better work.

John L. Sargent, in the opinion of those who think they know and have the right to judge, stands at the head of American portrait painters of the day. London, Paris, and New York have accepted the fiat of these self-constituted judges. The artist is now represented by six pictures, two of which are undoubtedly of surpassing merit as works of art. The large canvas of the "*Boit children*" leaves neither desire nor opportunity for criticism. It is so warm and rich in tone that it might have been painted by one of the Venetian masters of color. The children are charming in expression and pose. The painting is beyond all peradventure one of the most successful of those which in our days have attempted to depict childhood in the midst of luxurious surroundings. Indeed, the writer does not know where among the works of modern painters its superior in several respects is to be found. Next in merit is the portrait of "*Mme. W.*," a full length in white. It is simply composed, perfectly free from any attempt at boldness in effect, and gives us the idea of a woman of perfect breeding and refinement. Of the remaining four, that of "*Madam B.*" is the better, although it bears the unmistakable stamp of a society portrait, and of a woman who has perfect confidence in her "social position."

Julius L. Stewart is another of the successful Americans. He is the painter of thoroughly *chic* portraits of women, and works by a well conceived formula which always produces genteel results. He never paints a woman who appears to be of lower rank than that of baroness, and all his young girls look like the daughters of duchesses. It is unnecessary to say that his portraits are always acceptable to the sitters, as indeed they ought to be, for they are takingly composed, and as to general effect, perfectly genteel. His six works now exhibited show us an artist of more than ordinary ability, and thoroughly accomplished in a certain kind of technique. The prevailing defect in Mr. Stewart's portraits is the sameness of values. From top to bottom, and from side to side of the canvas, the same degree of distinctness is always visible. His "*Hunt ball*," which is regarded as his most notable work, is showy and original. It is a pretty picture of the world's airy nothings, engaged in an occupation which is taxing their intellects to the extreme of mental tension. The men in red coats beating tambourines, and the women so unexceptionally garbed, must remind all Americans of the dangerous and exciting anise-seed bag chase, and the "Hunt ball" of their only Newport. The artist, probably without intention, has produced a most telling satire. If he had spent a life time in experimenting, he could not have created a collection of more thoroughly vapid faces—fronts upon which vacancy enthroned sits supreme. The "*Hunt supper*" is a companion picture. "*Une Cour au Caire*" is a work of merit, and shows this artist at his best; but it is not one of his fashionable productions. "*La berge à Bougival*" is a river side scene in the outskirts of Paris, well composed, and fairly artistic in treatment.

Julian Russel Story exhibits three works, including a portrait of his father, which is one of the best in the American section. It is new to this period, but very old in its manner of color and free handling. The very large canvas by this artist represents *"Le Prince Noir trouvant le corps du roi de Bohême aprè la bataille de Crécy."* It is a most ambitious painting, but notwithstanding the fact that it is fairly well composed, it can not be regarded as a remarkable work of art.

Abbott Henderson Thayer has only one canvas, and this makes us regret that there are not more. It is *"Corps aile,"* an original and imaginative work, and one of the most charmingly painted heads in the whole Exhibition. It is a conception of rare refinement.

Wordsworth Thompson sends a canvas entitled *"Une ferme de New England."* It is a work of merit, and those who know the ground, with its peculiar associations and features, will recognize the truth of the picture.

G. S. Truesdell is likewise represented by a single painting, *"Le berger et son troupeau."* It is a quiet truthful picture of a shepherd and his sheep, of more than ordinary power.

Charles F. Ulrich has contributed his *"Dans la terre promise."* This, his best known and most ambitious work, depicts an everyday Castle Garden scene, filled with newly arrived emigrants. They are typical Germans seeking their earthly salvation in the new land of promise. The various types are well depicted, and the whole composition is wonderfully true.

Eugene L. Vail is a very strong painter of marine subjects, and his manner is peculiarly his own. He has his own way of looking at objects, and his own scheme of color. Of his four works in this Exhibition, the *"Porte de pêche, Concarneau,"* is very noteworthy. The subject is a fishing-smack with the wind on the port beam. Two men are at the ropes, and a third is steering. The boat is passing along the side of a wonderfully constructed wave-form in ponderous motion. The composition, the action, and the quality of color in this painting prove an artist of exceptional power. His other three works are strongly artistic, and are as distinctively his own as the one described.

Horatio Walker shows a strong bit of color in his *"Étable à cochons."* It is not an interesting subject, except perhaps to the mind of a pork-packer. To an ordinary person a pig sty is not a thing of beauty. but as a study of color and composition this work would do credit to George Morland.

E. L. Weeks is an artist who composes and paints from sketches made in the East. Since he has forsaken Egypt, India has seemingly been to him an inexhaustible field. The scenes of this country he contrives to bring in a most picturesque manner before the peoples of the West. He paints with rare fidelity and artistic effect, and it is doubtful if the works of any artist convey better pictures of Eastern life. One of his chief paintings, which is also among his latest, is "*Le dernier royage; souvenir du Gange.*" It shows the artist at his best. The view of the city of Benares is remarkable for masterly treatment of architectural effects. Two fakirs are crossing the Ganges in an open boat ; one is dying, and the other is using all haste so that his comrade may breathe his last on the sacred shore. The strange buildings, the water with its reflections, the Eastern costumes, and the brilliant Indian atmosphere, render this artistic composition extremely interesting.

J. Alden Weir exhibited three oil paintings. One, "*Portrait de l'enfant d'un artist,*" is a quaint picture in an old style, approaching the Dutch school, and none the worse for the resemblance. The other two—an example of still life, and a landscape, are likewise artistic, but of no particular force or art value.

PORTRAIT PAINTERS.

Among painters of portraits, whose work is fairly representative of the present condition of American art, may be mentioned the following exhibitors: Anderson, Mlle. Beaux, G. B. Butler, Cauldwell, Delachaux, Eakins, W. Eaton, Forbes, Healy, Hinckley, Huntington, Isham, Johnson, Mlle. Kellogg, Mme. Klumpke, Lockwood, Meza, Newman, Peters, Porter, Renouf, Rice, Strickland, Tarbell, Throop, Vonnoh, Wight, and Wiles.

LANDSCAPE PAINTERS.

Among the representative landscape painters who have sent works are, Benson, Boyden, Birch, Bristol, C. H. Eaton, Fisher, Gifford, Gross, Haas (Marine) H. Hamilton, J. M. Hart, Hassam, Hayden, Innes, Bolton Jones, MacEntee, Macy, Miller, Minor, Nicoll, Parton, Robbins, Van Boskerck, Whiteman, Whittridge, Wickenden, Ogden Wood, and Wyant. Several of these painters have devoted the better portion of their artistic careers to the delineation of American scenery, and have done so with success.

HISTORICAL AND GENRE PAINTERS.

The list of historical and *genre* painters does not contain many names that can be bracketed with notable works. The following, however, may be mentioned as having been fairly successful: Bacon, Baird, Birney, Blashfield, J. G. Brown, Darling, Denman, Dolph, Freer, Elizabeth Gardner, Hovenden, Irwin, Kavanah, Koehler, Millett, Moeller, Potthast, Ryder, Shirlaw, Stokes, Turner, Vedder, Volk, Ward, Webb, Witt, and T. W. Wood.

WATER COLORS AND DRAWINGS.

In the second class, which contains various original designs in water color, pen and ink, etc., the American exhibit is small but strong. At the head of the list, and among the first of his time stands Edward A. Abbey. He is a consummate master of graceful pose, costumes, and true elegance in composition. He moreover possesses the rare faculty of fixing upon a small surface the spirit and social tone of the period. Sheridan's immortal comedy, "School for Scandal," is not more remarkable in this respect than one of Abbey's drawings. He is a perfect master of the *technique* which serves him to elucidate his dainty creations. The work of this artist will stand the test of time as well as that of any of our great representative poets.

Charles S. Reinhart is also a notable draftsman, but in quite another direction from Abbey's. He is among those keen observers who content themselves with noting persons and things of to-day. He appears to perceive without difficulty an unknown side to the most commonplace object, and he has a happy and graphic way of presenting these commonplaces so as to make them amusing and interesting. He has fertility of imagination and the command of a facile pen.

The two pastel portraits by Julius L. Stewart are particularly interesting for graceful pose and simplicity of execution. Robert F. Blum, William H. Low, Fred Remington, Julius Rolshoven, Rosina E. Sherwood, William J. Whittemore, Kenyon Cox, J. Alden Weir, William H. Drake, Eliza Greatorex, Joseph Pennell, Irving W. Wiles, E. H. Blashfield, M. H. Gibson, A. C. Redwood, and several others are represented by very meritorious works.

SCULPTURE.

In the class of sculpture the American exhibit is insignificant as to numbers and weak artistically. S. H. Adams, has, however, a bust of a young girl which is thoroughly good work. It is free and sincere in treatment, and devoid of all littleness tending to detract from the dignity and effect of the whole.

Paul Wayland Bartlett contributes a purely ideal work "*Le Bohémien.*"—a full-length statue in bronze. A young man (nude) is teaching two little bears showman's tricks. In this group there is undoubted evidence of original design. The artist has something to say, and he has said it with masterly simplicity. The cubs show admirable study of character in animals. The silent protest of the one that is being taught, and the satisfaction of the other at having gotten through with its lesson, are expressed with consummate skill. The modelling of the man's figure, the attitude and expression of the face are excellent. For this work the artist was voted a

PLATE XI.

THE BOHEMIAN, BY BARTLETT.

sideration, and even then it was not quite settled in the minds of all
that exact justice had been done. This fact must be regarded as
most complimentary to the artistic merit of the whole collection.

FINLAND.

The contributions from Finland to the Exhibition, number seventy-
seven, of which fifty-seven are oil paintings. The exhibit as a
whole is not attractive or notable for artistic qualities. As a rule,
the endeavor to depict the beautiful is more observable in the
works of the Finnish artists than those of Danish painters; but
their art, although it may not be absolutely repulsive, is coarse and
unsympathetic.

FINNISH PAINTERS.

A. Edelfelt, who works in Paris, is an exception among his countrymen. He is a painter of rare power of expression and fidelity to
the best laws of art. His finer works go far in the direction of true
greatness. The one to be especially noticed of the ten he exhibits
is the full-length portrait of Pasteur in his laboratory, in the act of
examining the contents of a bottle which he holds in his hand. The
attitude and expression of mental absorption are perfectly portrayed,
and the great student stands before us in all the earnestness, dignity,
and simplicity of his character. "*La Vierge et l'enfant,*" is a work
of novel interest, for it gives a new interpretation of a much hack-
neyed subject. The scheme of color might with perfect propriety
be designated as spiritual, it is so light, transparent, and ethereal.
While it is the reverse of all that is solid in color, it is yet strongly
expressive. "*Au piano*" is another small work also delicate in
color, and the "*Portrait of Mme. S.*" proves that this artist has
much versatility in portraiture. The face in this picture is singularly expressive of a kindly nature and simplicity of character.

With the exception of "*Débarquement,*" by A. Jarnefelt, there is no
other picture in the Finnish section that seems to the writer worthy
of particular mention.

GREAT BRITAIN.

The contributions from Great Britain number five hundred and
fifty-two, and in each class there are to be found a sufficient number
of works by representative artists to give a fair idea of the present
state of the fine arts in the United Kingdom. In artistic qualities,
especially in all that relates to color, this section stands quite by
itself. In general composition and intention the exhibit is unlike
that of any other country. Among the oil paintings are to be perceived many attempts to imitate the depth, solidity, and warmth of
color so characteristic of the old Italian and Flemish masters. The
French gray, so much in vogue on the continent, has evidently not

reached the English side of the channel, but there is a clearly-defined British tendency in the direction of painting "pictures," such as delighted the readers of the "Annuals" forty years ago, and with which the catchpenny novels were garnished for many successive seasons. In this class of work the general texture is always velvety and highly colored—very blue eyes, very round, red cheeks, very red hair, very black hair, deep green grass, etc. Nature is ignored, but the picture is produced all the same. Notwithstanding this tendency there is a goodly proportion of historical and imaginative work, betokening studious research and an earnest striving for something above the uncouth realism so often depicted by continental artists. There is also some excellent work in black and white. Everything is pervaded by a spirit of perfect respectability. There are, to be sure, a few nudes of the strictly clothespin order, painted, as a rule, in such a repulsive and untruthful manner, and so far removed from any known nature, that they might be taken for nondescript divinities of an inconceivable world. No one would care to look at them a second time. But the presence of these creations does not affect the strictly moral aspect of the *tout ensemble,* and it is safe to say that in the whole English collection there is not a suggestion of unusual levity or a single touch of the brush that would "bring the blush of shame to the cheek of modesty." The triumph of the uses of art over immorality, either in suggestion or fact, is thorough and complete, and this, too, at a time when the temptation to be frivolous is so strong.

ENGLISH PAINTERS.

L. Alma-Tadema is among the better known of the artists now painting in England. He has worked in a particular field, and the reputation he has made has been won within narrow limits. He is now represented by two oil paintings and two water colors. Of the oils, "*Les femmes d'Amphissa,*" important as to subject and size, is in his peculiar style. It is largely composed of female figures in Greek dress, and was suggested by a passage in "Daniel Deronda." It seems a painting without a purpose; no definite idea is expressed, and there is no central point of interest. The women are scattered all over the canvas. Those who face the spectator are English girls in ancient costume, and those shown in profile have much the same massive lines which form the head on the present American dollar. The picture is not remarkable for truthfulness of color, and several of the figures are too long. It has neither national color nor local flavor, and were it not for the costumes, this representation would stand for Gaul quite as well as for Greece. If it had been painted by an unknown artist, it would be pronounced a thoughtless "studio" picture; but having the name of a *great* artist attached to it, we are perforce compelled to call it a great work. The other oil by this artist,

"*L'Attente*" is a single figure, and is likewise marked by his peculiarities.

E. Burne Jones is another English artist who does not work in beaten paths, and there is much diversity of opinion respecting the merit of his pictures. That he is, as to this period, original, there can be no doubt whatever; but the value of his originality from an art standpoint is an open question. His single contribution to this collection "*Le Roi Cophetua*," is to the ordinary human intelligence a mystery. Possibly there may be a supremely enlighted one capable of interpreting its hidden meaning, for doubtless he has one which does not appear on the surface. It purports to tell the story of a king, who, disregarding the rights and traditions of royalty, is in the act of offering his crown to a beautiful beggar girl. But the picture seems to be in three parts on a single canvas. There are two dark brown heads at the top, representing chorister boys, a full length figure in the middle with death white arms and face devoid of expression, and another dark brown, almost black face at the bottom, all false in color and untruthfully drawn. The *ensemble* forces the conviction that the artist tried to paint a pre-Raphael picture. Altogether it is elaborate, devoid of dignity, and has the appearance of a recently discovered design for an ancient glass window; but its worst feature is its pretentiousness. It has the incorrect drawing of the pre-Raphael period without the color, and is so ornate with trivial details that it has none of the dignity of the works of those days, and like a proposition in several sorts of later poetry, needs an explanation. An eminent French critic has intimated that this artist is a follower of Mantegna.

J. P. Calderon has sent a sent a little canvas entitled "*Aphrodite.*" A fairly drawn and very solid nude figure is floating upon very blue water, with a rather lazy, graceful movement.

E. Crofts contributes "*Marlborough après la bataille de Ramillies.*" It is an earnest attempt to give a view of a camp scene after a fight, but it is not a success if judged from the De Neuville standard. It lacks the dirt, character, and movement of an army of fighting men.

Luke Fildes is represented by three works, all of the picture-book. colored-plate order, in which are to be found several sets of very white even teeth, round red, brown, and white faces, round black eyes, and florid costumes. "*Venetiennes*" is eminently one of this kind. The others show the same qualities in a lesser degree.

Stanhope A. Forbes, in his "*Société philharmonique de village*" presents a scene in the everyday life of an English village. a vocal and instrumental rehearsal. It is a character work, and the English types are well marked. The action is good, and the whole is fairly composed. The artist's other work, "*Une famille de nomades,*" is less successful.

Andrew C. Gow is represented by a very carefully painted and well composed war picture, "*La garnison défilant avec les honneurs de la guerre, Lille,* 1798." This is a thoroughly honest work and shows considerable skill for composition and picturesque outline. The group of mounted officers is well constructed, the men and horses carefully—a little too carefully—painted, and the battalion passing in front of them is fairly on the move. This artist, however, has made the common mistake of nearly all painters of war scenes, the men are too well dressed and too clean. The dirt and atmosphere of war are not portrayed.

H. Herkomer contributes two portraits of handsome women, one in white, the other in black. There can be no doubt about these being striking likenesses of the persons they represent. They are in several respects among the most thoroughly pleasing portraits in the Exhibition. In their broad and simple treatment they come very near to what is good in art. But the great volume and marble-like massiveness of the drapery of the one in white, and the grandiose pose of the other are the regrettable defects in these works.

The late Frank Holl is represented by a portrait of Sir H. Rawlinson. It is strong in color and drawing, lifelike in expression, and almost free from disturbing efforts at effect. One such blemish, however, in this otherwise excellent work, is a patch of red drapery on the left arm of the chair.

J. C. Hook, a marine painter and a colorist far above the average, has three works. "*Le départ pour le phare,*" and "*A quelque chose malheur est bon,*" are both paintings of decided merit. In each the effect of atmosphere is clearly indicated, and the wave movements are strongly depicted. The third painting is not so successful. The introduction or poorly executed human figures into the works of this artist mar the generally fine effect of their simple outline.

W. B. Leader is a landscape painter of ability. He is represented by a work entitled "*Sur le soir il y aura de la lumière.*" It is a broadly handled and luminous study from nature, and is executed in a manner that shows correct knowledge of atmospheric and outdoor effect generally.

Sir Frederick Leighton, president of the Royal Academy, and one of the most known among living English artists, has sent three paintings to the Exhibition. The largest of these, and the one that appears to represent his most serious attempt is "*Andromaque Captive.*" Imagine a large canvas covered with semiarchaic figures in several colors, "attitudinizing." The females are all of one family, with faces, hair, and expression as alike as possible, and clothed in porcelain robes of pronounced green, blue, red, yellow, and white, ample and voluminous ; the nudes painted copperish brown, and all of these figures scattered over a canvas, or grouped in a way that betrays no intelligent purpose, and some idea of this extraordinary picture may be formed. Several of the women are possessed of water jugs, and seemingly engaged in the occupation of carrying water, but their costumes, poses, and demeanor indicate that they are of the higher cast of Epirus society. Possibly it may have been painted with the intention of remotely imitating Pompeiian decoration, but what we know of that ancient art is in favor of its directness and simplicity, whereas Sir Frederick Leighton's work is enormously pretentious. It is an arbitrary production without local color, and represents Rome quite as much as Epirus. In the opinion of the writer it is an extreme presentation by a formalist, and is related in a very limited sense to natural objects. "*Simœta, la sorcière*" is a work of the same order, but the portrait of Lady Coleridge comes a little nearer the earth, and is altogether more satisfactory.

Sir John Millais is perhaps the most "successful" of living English painters. His works are very much sought after in England, and command high prices. Of his six pictures now exhibited, his portrait of Gladstone is the most complete and satisfactory. It is a profile, three-quarters length, on a dark background, and is painted in strict accordance with the best rules of portraiture. The face is expressive, the head well modeled, and the pose perfectly natural. Another portrait by this artist, that of Mr. J. C. Hook, is very different, in treatment, especially as to color, and might have been painted by anybody. "*Les Cerises*" is a pleasing picture of a child in "old English" dress. There is a decidedly old English air about the whole composition. "*Cendrillon*" is a figure simpler in execution, and less indebted to costume and surroundings for its value as a work of art.

Henry Moore is undoubtedly one of the very small number of good marine painters of his time. His two works "*Après la pluie le beau temps,*" and "*La malle de New-Haven,*" are excellent examples of his style. The first is the most attractive on account of the crisp effect of atmosphere, and the pure blue of the water. The sky is of a brilliant, transparent gray, and were it not for a rather heavy streak of dark cloud hanging over the fore center of the painting, and which seems to have no business there, the picture would be as nearly as possible a perfect work of art. As it is, it is a most remarkable production. The other canvas does not impress one so favorably, but it is nevertheless characteristic of the fine work of this artist.

W. Q. Orchardson is a distinguished painter with strong and well founded pretensions to be considered a colorist; his tones are unusually deep and warm, and in his finer works he is very exact in his relations and tone gradations. Of his three paintings now exhibited, "*Tout seul*" is a striking example of the marked characteristics of his better work. Every touch of the brush indicates a wholly intelligent purpose. The entire composition shows minute elabora- '

tion, but upon the broadest possible lines. How quietly, but how wonderfully, does this picture express the idea of "all alone!" "*Sa première danse,*" a charming and daintily painted canvas, depicts a dancing lesson early in the century. Very much of the effect is gained by a faithful delineation of the costumes of the period. "*Maître bébé*" is not so interesting as either of the others.

W. W. Ouless exhibits two portraits. That of Cardinal Manning is a wonderful success in the direction of careful and effective elaboration. The ecclesiastical red robe and the ermine cape are difficult elements to manage in a portrait. In this instance they have been so artistically handled as not to detract from the dignity of the whole. The face is a marvel of successful modeling. This is a show portrait in the best sense of the term.

Alfred Parsons has contributed two landscapes. "*Aux bords du Shannon*" may be regarded as a successful work. The foreground has been very carefully painted, and the general perspective is good. The other canvas, "*Étude d'hiver,*" is merely a study.

John R. Reid is represented by two very interesting works, "*Rivalité entre grands-pères*" and "*Sans toit.*" They are both story-telling pictures. In the first, are two grandfathers showing a little girl how to look through a "spy-glass." In the second, is a family group of strolling musicians—man, woman, and child, out of luck. In each case the story is well told. "*Sans toit*" is especially descriptive; the old clarionet player looks so cold, so pinched, and unhappy; the grown-up daughter so weary and thoughtful, and her little child so timid and shrinking from the world. A lot of happy children have encountered this sad band and are looking at them with pitying eyes. In both works we have good composition and excellent *technique*.

Briton Rivière has two canvases. One, "*N'éveillez pas le chien qui dort,*" is a remarkable presentation of a pair of thorough brutes—a bulldog and a brute man. The latter is *sui generis*, and can not be found in any country out of communication with the British Isles. He is sleeping with the dog—the more human of the two. But although the face of this man is in repose its lines indicate the murderer, the prizefighter, the wife-beater, and the burglar. The other work, "*Chez le magicien,*" is a carefully-wrought interior, where, among other objects, we see two leopards. The picture is not particularly interesting.

J. J. Shannon exhibits a good portrait of Henry Vigne; quiet in color, dignified and natural in pose, and well treated generally.

John M. Swan has a picture of a lioness defending her cubs, treated with a very free hand. The drawing is excellent, but the tone is so dark that the merits of good composition are hardly discernible.

G. F. Watts is always an original painter. He has created a world of his own and peopled it with abnormal beings. When he has thought out a new composition, he draws from this ample storehouse and fills his canvas with his own unrealities. He seems to have a strong liking for long, nude women. They are all constructed upon the same formula, and are 10½ heads long. In "*Le jugment de Paris*" there are three of these in a row, facing the spectator and standing (strictly) at attention. "*L'Amour et la vie*" has another. "*Hope*" is represented by a blue young woman, "doubled up," seated on the world, and nearly covering it with her ample length. "*Mammon*" is typified by a huge monster, something between a German idea of the devil and a Porte St. Martin theater stage fiend, very big and very red, sitting in a chair, with his right foot on the top of a nude manikin and another clutched with his right hand. This is a very terrible affair, and is undoubtedly the hardest hit Mammon has ever received. Four other works by this artist are exhibited. No one can question their originality.

J. McNeil Whistler is another of the world's exceptional beings. He writes, etches, draws, and paints, and was born in the United States. He has been before the world in his several capacities since 1863, and so managed his affairs as to command his full share of public attention. In relation to his art work there is the greatest possible divergence of opinion. To-day one critic exhausts the list of complimentary adjectives and high-flown terms—"art-critic"* jargon—to describe the poetry, the hidden, subtle charm, the delicate suggestiveness, the grace, etc., of his work; to-morrow, another critic, quite as well informed, will exhaust the opposite set of adjectives, and coin terms more remarkable for strength than elegance to denounce the sham, pretense, and transparent humbug of Mr. Whistler's work. Thus the doctor's disagree, and the truth probably lies somewhere between these opposite views. It may be said without hesitation of this painter that his perceptions are far from being those of the ordinary artist; that his ideas as to how natural objects should be represented upon canvas are quite his own. His work is often supremely affected, often daintily and charmingly

---

* A SPECIMEN.

Corot, the most exquisite of idealists, because his art is firmly based on and generalized from nature, lovingly and *endlessly observed*, may be counted among France's most truly classic masters. *There is in his best work a reticence, a gentle melancholy, not divorced from hope*, which exercises on the beholder an influence akin to that of fine Greek art; in mastery of composition, artful in its seeming simplicity, he has in France no rival; not even Claude Lorraine himself, who possessed the art but not the artlessness.

Corot did not "endlessly observe." It is a notorious fact that during the last years of his life he painted "studio" pictures and saw very little of nature. His best are consummate works of art, filled with poetic sentiment, and are often very far off from nature. But where comes in "a reticence, a gentle melancholy, not divorced from hope?"

The above is not very far away from the average art writing of to-day. For the balance of the article see New Review for September, 1889.

incorrect, and his best and most sincere productions are only suggestive of what a complete painting ought to be. It may be asserted that the majority of his efforts are suggestive conceits rather than earnestly executed work.

Among the English oil paintings Mr. Whistler has two examples; "*Portrait de Lady Archibald Campbell; arrangement en noir No. 7,*" and "*Le balcon; harmonie couleur chair et couleur verts.*" The portrait is truly Whistlerarian, and in no respect satisfactory. The subject is neither walking nor standing. A rudimentary foot is shown, but it seems to be suspended from something and incapable of bearing weight; it is not an English foot, nor does it even appear to rest on anything. It is only an incorrect suggestion of a foot. The figures is top-heavy with the unpicturesque rotundity of a fur cape which gives to the subject something of the appearance of an inverted irregular pyramid. At the top of the structure is a head with no indication of a neck, and nearly the whole is an arrangement in black—or rather an affectation in various shades of dark mud. The other work is a charming conceit in delicacy of color, and graceful ease of composition. It is manufactured out of the whole cloth of the artist's imagination and makes no pretension to truthfulness. The costumes, tea tray, musical instrument, and balcony are Japanese, but the faces of the girls are English, and the tall smokestacks of Thames manufactories appear on the opposite side of the river. The picture is a singular mixture, but a most fascinating one.

WATER COLORS.

The English display of water colors is large and comprehensive, and thoroughly national in its leading characteristics, the chief of which is careful elaboration in imitation of solid oil painting. Among those whose works appear to have been executed more in accord with the generally admitted theory of what water color drawings ought to be, as practiced by the artists of other nations, may be mentioned the names of J. Aumonier, W. Langley, H. Marshall, and W. L. Wyllie. There is one work "*Un nouveau quartier de Londres,*" by Alfred East, which is of remarkable merit. It is in fact one of the best water colors in the whole Exposition.

SCULPTURE.

The sculpture exhibit of the English is not imposing. The conceptions of the English sculptors are not clearly and boldly set forth, and their subjects are complicated and difficult to understand. They are seemingly fully alive to the value of the simple Greek lines, but do not know quite how to portray them. "*Reveil,*" by Sir Frederick Leighton, is a case in point. This statue of a man stretching and

H. Ex. 410—VOL 2——6

yawning has many good points illustrating action and expression, but is another very clear specimen of "attitudinizing," and very defective in its technical development. The statuette by the same artist, entitled "*Fausse Alarme*," is that of a girl looking over her shoulder with an expression of fear, the cause of her alarm being a toad on the ground. There is much that is pleasing in this work, but it does not convey the idea of great power.

Hamo Thornycroft's "*Teucer*" is serious in subject and treatment, and altogether sculpturesque. The movement is vigorous and simple, but loses in strength by sameness of values. It is, however, very interesting by its conception, which recalls the antique, and it is by far the best piece of sculpture in the English section.

ETCHINGS.

Among the fine etchings to be found in this section is to be noticed the work of Hayden, R. W. Macbeth, Short, Whistler, and others. The nine by Whistler are characteristic, that is to say, supremely airy and artistic suggestions of substantial objects. They convey an idea of uncertainty and atmosphere seldom found in such works.

GREECE.

The Greek section, including the five classes, contains ninety-one items, and with the exception of two statues, one of Paris, the other of a Greek slave, by Bounanos, of Athens, there is nothing worthy of mention. In the whole list of forty-six paintings in oil, there is not to be found a single canvas which calls for serious consideration. The two statues referred to are only fair specimens of conventional work. In the one of Paris, an attempt to produce a body after the antique is perceptible, but the head is that of an Italian officer of to-day. The decline of art in the most classic of all lands seems to be complete and final, *i. e.*, if the display of modern Greek art at this Exhibition be comprehensive and representative.

ITALY.

The official catalogue states the number of works from Italy to be three hundred and twenty-seven, but owing to mistakes of the compiler or to very late arrivals, the actual number is greater in each class. As a whole, the Italian collection is not an encouraging one, and after looking carefully through it one naturally asks, what has become of the artistic instinct of the Italians which is supposed to be so national? Has the influence of the great Renaissance disappeared and left no trace upon the later Italian artists?

The work of the present day shows neither strength of imagination, correct composition, nor dignity, and were it not for a few landscapes and a small number of figure compositions, the collection would be hardly worthy of notice. Nothing in art could be more dreary, trifling, and devoid of interest than a large majority of the figure pieces, which as a rule, both as to value of subject and execution, do not reach above the level of the hundred thousand times gaudily painted Roman peasant, male and female, with which the world has been so bountifully supplied during the last seventy-five years. The absence of skillful *technique* is quite as apparent as are the faults of composition, and it may be said of the whole collection that if it indicates anything, it is a want of ambition, and tendency to be satisfied with very trivial results.

PAINTINGS IN OIL.

Leonardo Bazzaro, of Milan, is represented by two really strong and characteristic works. One, called "*Chioggia*," is a Venetian composition of water architecture and figures. The scheme of color is warm, deep, and strong, and the action of the women crossing a bridge is natural and easy. The other canvas, "*Couvent*," is a vigorous landscape with an old convent in the foreground. These are among the few really fine works in the Italian section.

Bartholomeo Bezzi, of Rome, exhibits a landscape, "*Les bords d'une rivière.*" It is a fair example of warm color, and shows some very broad and comprehensive drawing.

Jean Boldini, probably the best known of the Italian artists of this time, is represented by nine works. Two portraits of men, one of whom is Verdi, are remarkably lifelike. That of the great composer is especially so; it is strong to coarseness, but is the counterfeit of the actual man. There are also three full-length portraits of women which are decidedly original in a certain sense. The scheme of color in regard to drapery is greenish white, and in relation to flesh, ash gray, while in each case the figure resembles in form an elongated pyramid. These portraits can not be regarded seriously, but if viewed from the standpoint of sensationalism, then success to the verge of grotesqueness is unquestionable.

Filippo Carcano contributes three landscapes. "*Lac d'Iseo*," with snow-topped mountains in the distance and a lake'in the foreground, has a fine atmospheric effect. The others are "*Le coucher du soleil*," fairly well painted, with strong Italian characteristics, and "*La plaine Lombarde*," a broad and comprehensive view, but not satisfactory as to color.

Guglielmo Ciardi is represented by four landscapes, two of these, "*Torrent, vallée de Primiero*," and "*Octobre*," are of especial merit. They are faithful and picturesque transcriptions from nature, and prove that the artist is both a master of *technique* and a careful and intelligent student of scenery.

Angelo Morbelli, of Milan, has but a single work, "*Les derniers jours*," but it is one of the thoroughly suggestive works of the Exhibition, and realizes much that is most simple and straightforward in art. It depicts a large room in a charitable institution for old men in Milan. The inmates are seated in long rows facing in one direction, with a most suggestive expression of waiting on all their faces— waiting for bodily sustenance, perhaps, and for the peace of death that is not far off. All the heads are carefully painted, and all express in a variety of ways the supreme thought the picture is intended to represent.

G. Muzzioli has a work which is not given in the catalogue. It contains some painting of old marbles, quite remarkable for the success with which it imitates the softness to be observed on the very ancient ones of Rome. There are two figures fairly well done, but treated in the later Italian fashion.

Luigi Nono exhibits a work called *"Fruitier,"* which gives us the interior of a vegetable and fruit shop in the charge of a girl who has a younger child with her. Nothing could be more realistic than the painting of the vegetables and fruit, and the figures in the shop are as thoroughly Italian as possible. This may not be high art, but of its kind it is excellent.

Giovanni Segantini, of Milan, is a painter possessing very strong individuality. Of the three canvases he exhibits, one is a study of horses, another of cows, and the third of sheep. He draws with an exactitude seldom seen, the action of his animals is natural, and his landscape is scrupulously correct; yet with all these qualities his work does not leave much impression on the beholder. There is a certain hardness of texture that prevents it from being of the taking sort. His paintings are merely interesting examples of very conscientious work.

Adolfo Tommassi is another of the fairly good Italian artists who paint in a characteristic manner. His two landscapes are full of the atmosphere and the forms of Italy. *"Après la gelée,"* is a perfectly artistic rendering of wonderful frostbitten nature. A field of withered cabbages would not in a general way affect the imagination, but here the artist has succeeded in giving them such a forlorn appearance that sympathy is excited, and one feels real sorrow for the dead cabbages.

PASTELS.

Among the pastels are two by Arturo Reitti, of more than ordinary excellence.

SCULPTURE.

Among the ninety-eight contributors to the sculpture class, there is hardly a single piece showing on the part of the artist the slightest appreciation of the dignity and grandeur of the great art adorned by the works of Donatello and a long list of illustrious Italian masters. The majority of the pieces do not reach far above the artistic standard of the trivial mantle ornaments which may be purchased in the shops of the poorest bronze founders. They have the usual embellishments, which constitute the well-known tricks of the stone-cutter's trade for fascinating the eye of those who have a taste for millinery in marble, and they ought to be set down as mere articles of commerce, and never be measured by any known standard applied to art. Exception may possibly be made in the case of two or three busts, and the foregoing statements certainly do not apply to several of the works of Eugenio Maccagnani, of Rome. This artist exhibits five miniature busts in bronze which are in perfect imitation of the Greek, but are at the same time original and strongly characteristic of the sculptor. The general handling is marked by perfect freedom from the conventional, and shows considerable aptitude for interpret-ing nature. It is to be regretted that his successful little studies were not enlarged to the size of life.

NORWAY.

The exhibits from Norway number one hundred and forty-three items, of which one hundred and twenty-five are oil paintings. Although the work of the Norwegian painters collectively does not rank very high when measured by the standard of what is best in art, the section contains much that is original and interesting. Even among the almost rudimentary attempts there are to be found earnestness of purpose and vigorous brush work, and the general tendency is to go very close to nature, and to imagine as little as possible.

The subjects in the story-telling works are, as a rule, selected from scenes in low life, and the point of chief interest is usually devel-oped with simplicity and directness of aim, sometimes showing appreciation of sentiment and capacity for expressing it. The *technique* is usually coarse, but it is frequently telling and very much to the point.

PAINTINGS IN OIL.

Mlle. Harriet Backer is represented by two works. The one entitled *"Chez moi"* is a pleasant composition in gray of a young woman at a piano. It is simple and effective. The second canvas is less successful.

Jacob Bratland gives a little domestic story of parents watching over a sick child. It is earnest and true without pretension.

Jacob Gloersen contributes *"Au bois,"* a very careful, strong study of a May day in the woods. The forms are well drawn and all the natural relations are faithfully preserved.

Hans Heyerdahl exhibits three canvases. His *"Soir d'été"* is a very strong and thoroughly masculine work. It has the coarse, vigorous qualities of the north. The perspective is well managed. In *"Deux soeurs"* we have two thoroughly Scandinavian young faces, as blond and honest as possible. One is beautiful and unearthly pure, to the point of the angelic.

Mlle. Kitty Kielland has four canvases. One, *"Après la pluie,"* perfectly conveys the picture of a wet bit of country after rain.

Christian Krohg is a realistic painter of stubborn facts. In his line of panels, *"Trois générations"* we see the first, second, and third of one of the rough seafaring households of the sturdy north folk. The wonderful ugliness of the old heads is depicted even to the utmost depth of the last wrinkle. They are all very interesting, but chiefly because we know that they are perfectly true. Two *genre* works are of the same character, but not so successful, for the reason that the artist tried to mix some imagination with his paint, and failed.

Gerhard Munthe is a landscape painter who can give to his works the real outdoor feeling. Of his three pictures, *"Jour d' été"* is the most successful. It depicts a scene with character, and conveys the true impression of a summer day.

Eilip Peterson is another realist who sticks honestly to nature in a coarse, strong way, but among his three pieces is one, *"Nuit d' été,"* full of genuine sentiment as well as individuality.

Christian Skredevig has a large canvas, *"Le soir de St. Jean en Norvège."* In this scheme of dark green, a mountain is hiding the sun from the water, but it is not sunset. The composition is true to nature, and conveys a good idea of a late Norwegian afternoon among the mountains. *"Monte Aventino"* is a pictorial Italian architectural piece, showing a fine appreciation of local atmosphere and color, and a correct perspective. *"Une ferme à Venoix"* is a rustic piece with peasants and cows, correct, strong, and unrefined.

Fritz Thaulow is possibly the better of the living Norwegian painters. His *"L'attente"* is a simple bit of out-of-doors scenery, with a horse attached to an open wagon, waiting at a gate. It is a little subject, not particularly interesting in itself, but is treated in such a pleasant, natural way that it compels admiration. *"Hiver en Norvège,"* and *"Un dimanche ; après le service,"* are fine examples of the successful delineation of winter scenes. We feel through them the calm, staying cold of the far north. The frostiness of the air is so perceptible that in looking at these works one is disposed to shiver. The two pastels, *"Marais"* and *"Le dégel"* are original and artistic, the latter especially so.

Erek Werenskiold is an artist of rare power over the most direct methods of expression. His *"Deux frères"*—an interior with an infant in the cradle, and an older brother sleeping in a chair near to it—is a very homely subject made interesting by artistic treatment. *"Grandemère"* is a plain, unvarnished truth. This portrait conveys the idea of a really kind and estimable grandmother. "*Paysage*" is a very tender and truthful study from nature. "*Enterrement à la campagne*" is, like the others, a simple transcript from the actual The newly opened grave, the reading of the last service, and the sorrowful reverence of the mourners, are faithfully depicted. All of these works are pitched in a high key of color, and the lighter tones are particularly tender and transparent.

HOLLAND.

Holland is represented by two hundred and eighty-eight exhibits, and outside of the two hundred and seventeen oil paintings there are not many works of marked merit or of special interest. Even among the oils, the work generally is not of a high order. The decadence is not so marked or so far advanced as it is in Italy, if the works now exhibited fairly represent the condition of the arts of both countries. There seems to be more ambition, more serious effort, in Holland, but it can be plainly seen that the skill which is taught by the training school is wanting. The composition of the figure pieces especially, is usually of the commonplace, book-illustration order, and the execution is inexact and unskillful. There are, however, several strong and accomplished artists among the exhibitors, and their work is worthy of consideration.

PAINTINGS IN OIL.

D. A. C. Artz is represented by three canvases. One, "*Consolation*," is fine in sentiment and well composed, but is not all that could be desired in color; the tones are not clear and decisive. The others may be passed over.

Nicholas Bastert has a large study of Autumn, very rich in color. It is not one of the gaudy autumnal pictures, for the tones are deep as well as warm. The whole is painted with a free hand.

Georges H. Breitner contributes a clever, sketchy advance of cavalry line. The movement is correct, and the general effect like the reality.

Edouard Frankfort has sent an interesting work entitled "*Une leçon du Talmud.*" We have here a well drawn group of the Teacher and His followers—Jews of the intellectual sort are eagerly listening to the great history so intimately connected with their past.

P. J. C. Gabriel is an artist of rather strong individuality, and one of his three exhibits, "*Une tourbière en Overijssel*," must be representative of his better work. The ruling qualities are breadth of treatment, atmosphere, and perspective.

Joseph Israels, probably the best known as well as the most gifted of contemporary Dutch painters, exhibits three works. "*Les travailleurs de la mer*" is painted in a very large and vigorous manner. The water has the true movement of the ocean, and the two sea-

faring men, carrying the anchor and rope, are very natural figures.
"*Paysans à table*" has the same sterling qualities. Sincerity and a
fine appreciation of color are strong elements in the works of this
painter.

Frederic H. Kraemmerer is a Dutch artist who has painted in
Paris for many years, and his works are so well known that any
description of them would be superfluous here. It will be sufficient
to say that they are costume, incident, and character pictures of the
French revolutionary period: and treated as he treats it, it may be
said that he has had the field quite to himself. He is entitled to the
credit of having vividly recalled the dress, the grotesque vagaries,
and the follies of a most extraordinary period.

Two works by Henry Luyten, "*Déjeuner d'ouvriers*" and "*Une
séance de si je puis*," show greater facility for composition than
capacity for correct execution. The paintings, however, are meritorious and not without interest.

The five canvases by Jacob Maris indicate considerable capacity
in several directions. In landscape and architectural painting he is
equally at home, without being great in either. He sees nature with
the eye of a true artist, and usually succeeds in avoiding the error
of overelaboration; but his finished pictures are uneven. If he
succeeds in tone, he fails in perspective, etc. The best of his five
pieces is "*La vieille bonne*," which is well composed and strongly
painted.

Anton Mauve, who died in 1888, is represented by five works, all
painted with a free hand. The forms are sketchy and light, very
artistic in touch; the color is tender and truthful. The work entitled
Bruyère is of marked excellence, something in the style of Michel,
but freer in thé drawing.

Hendrik Willem Mesdag has the quality of individuality more
marked than any other Dutch painter of his time. His works are, so
to speak, signed all over, so as to be quite unmistakable. "*À l'ancre*"
and "*Marée montante*" are good examples of strong, sober painting.
In the first, the floating ships are remarkably drawn. In both the
perspective and tone are excellent. The third, "*Nuit au bord de la
mer à Scheveningue*," is a moonlight scene of exceptional interest. It
has the merit of successful perspective, such as is seldom equaled in
the treatment of this aspect of nature, so difficult to paint.

Albert Neuhuys is a *genre* painter. He is represented by five
works. In the scale of art they do not rank very high. They are
somewhat original, fairly composed, but indifferent in execution.
The best of the number are "*Le cordonnier du village*" and "*Moments
de peine.*"

Willem Roelofs is a delineator of Dutch scenes, which he treats
with considerable success. Of the three now exhibited, "*Polder à
Noorden en Hollande*" is the most complete and artistic both as to

drawing and color. The prevailing tone is gray, but more transparent than the usual gray of continental painters.

Mlle. Therese Schwartze is a young artist of much promise. She has undoubtedly a fine instinct for color and artistic pose. Of her three canvases, her portrait of herself in working costume is by far the best. It is original, broad in treatment, and must be a strong likeness.

WATER COLORS, ETCHINGS, AND DRAWINGS IN BLACK AND WHITE.

Among the water colorists and workers in black and white, may be mentioned the names of Bock, Bosboom, Cate, and Weissenbrach, who are represented by fairly good contributions. Among the Dutch etchers whose work is far above the average, may be found the names of Vith, Witsen, and Zilken.

SCULPTURE.

There are only two pieces of sculpture in the Dutch section; both are uninteresting.

RUSSIA.

Of the two hundred and five works contributed by Russian artists to the various classes, one hundred and forty-six are oil paintings. It can not be said of the whole collection that it takes a high place among those of other European countries. While it includes a few works of considerable interest, and decidedly meritorious from an art standpoint, it must be acknowledged that the majority rise only to the level of commercial commonplace, and if artistic at all must be regarded as belonging to the category of the ornamental rather than the intellectually aesthetic. Careless and incorrect composition clearly proving the want of intelligent appreciation of the forms and resources of natural objects, and the absence of skillful *technique* are plainly observable in many of the works of the Russian painters in oil.

PAINTINGS IN OIL.

By the death of Mlle. Marie Bashkirtzeff not only her own country but the world of art sustained the loss of a unique character. She was a painter of much promise, possessing the art instinct to a wonderful degree, and being especially endowed with the faculty of reproducing the expression of the human face. Her ten works now exhibited afford ample evidence of this. The " *Portrait*," " *Sous le parapluie*," " *Pierre et Jacques* " (two boys on their way to school), " *Le rive*," in three panels, showing an infant, a girl of ten, and one of sixteen, each in the act of laughing, prove that the artist's success with commonplace subjects is to be summed up in three words— truthfulness, directness of purpose, and simplicity of execution.

"*Un atelier de peinture*" shows, like the others, the perfection of honest endeavor and appreciation of natural forms.

Joseph Chelmonski is an artist of prodigious individuality of the right sort. He rejoices in painting the peasants and horses of his country. His "*Marché aux chevaux*" is as national as possible, that is to say, thoroughly Russian. The atmosphere, the rush of the magnificent horses full of splendid action and animal life, their keepers, and the groups of buyers and sellers bargaining, are all faithfully spread before us. "*Un dimanche en Pologne*" is a work of rare strength and originality. In this scene of peasants junketing out of doors are fully depicted the robust, boisterous, and rude pleasures of an untutored class who hold on to the old manners and customs of their ancestors. In this composition it is difficult to decide which to admire most—the wonderful scheme of deep, strong color, the grouping of the figures, the action, or the sky or landscape. The artist is one of the very few who have mastered the extremes of physical action. The movements of his men and animals always seem to be perfectly natural, whereas in the works of other artists they are often forced and grotesquely exaggerated. His two other paintings are fit companions to those above described.

Jean Endogouroff contributes a canvas depicting a very cold Russian night, with a good perspective, which in such works is rare. Two others, "*L'Automne en Crimée*" and "*Le soir*," are well composed and very characteristic of the painter.

Alexis Harlamoff is an artist of some individuality, and his work is of the pleasing order. He has facility for producing agreeably decorative effects of color, but the power of composition is not his. Of his eleven subjects, seven are entitled "*Tête d'enfant.*" They may have been intended for different infants' heads, but they are substantially alike. In position, costume, color, etc., they scarcely differ one from the other.

Samuel Hirszenberg is represented by a very dark interior, containing a well composed group. It is a serious attempt to illustrate the intellectual side of the Jewish character.

Kouznetzoff, of Odessa, contributes one work, "*Devant l'autorité*," a characteristically Russian scene. An official, in an open carriage with attendants, is listening to the complaints of a group of country people. The composition is pictorial, and character is well depicted in the different faces.

Georges Lehmann is a portrait painter, and three of his six works exhibited are portraits. One of his canvases, "*Dame; sous le Directoire*," is noteworthy on account of its original and artistic treatment. It might be termed a study in blue, that being the dominant color. The composition is taking and graceful and the *technique* is skillful.

Constantine Makouski is an ambitious and inventive painter, but he has not sufficient grasp of *technique* to give adequate expression to his creations. His large canvas "*Jugement de Paris*," is pitched in a very high key of color, is purely decorative and conventional, but has some rather artistic and graceful details. His "*Mort d'Ivan-le-Terrible*" has, in regard to color, all the qualities of the chromo. His five exhibits afford convincing evidence that he would rank well as an artist if he only knew how to *paint*.

Joseph Pankiewicz exhibits one work, "*Marché aux légumes; Varsovie*," which is a vividly realistic picture of a vegetable market, with figures exceedingly characteristic of the place and people; but the subject appears to be hardly worth the labor bestowed upon it.

Ivan Pranishnikoff contributes nine small works in oil. This artist has a sense of the beautiful in composition and color. His faculty for construction enables him to make a thing of conventional beauty out of the most commonplace natural objects. His forms are light and graceful, and his colors conventional but warm. His work is notable for the qualities which generally please. It is rather singular that some enterprising dealer has not started a specialty under the name of "The Pranishnikoff gems."

Swiedomski, of Kieff, is represented by a very large canvas, "*Épisode de la Terreur*." It is a very spirited composition. A crowd of wild revolutionists, of both sexes, armed, and wearing the florid dress of the period, rushing away from a broken carriage and the body of a beautiful woman whom they have murdered and left upon the road. The story is vividly told, and recalls the terrible period of which this scene is only an "episode."

Vinceslas Szymanowski proves conclusively by his single picture, "*Rixe de montagnards polonais dans un cabaret*," that he is an artist of unusual power. For color, drawing of the human figure, facial expression, and natural action this work is truly remarkable. All that is involved in a peasant's quarrel—energetic gesticulation, infuriated faces, involuntary movements of anger, violent language—is forcibly expressed, without exaggeration. The masterly composition of this large canvas compels attention.

WATER COLORS, PASTELS, AND DRAWINGS.

In class 2, water colors, pastels, black and white, etc., there is some very good work by Adalbert Gerson, Pranishnikoff—who contributes much that is varied and in his best vein—Samokich, and Pierre Sokoloff, whose large water color of "*Marché aux chevaux*" is most noteworthy. The composition is true to nature, and great skill is shown in the execution.

SCULPTURE.

The Russian sculpture is not strong either in quantity or quality. It can not be said to bear any national impress, but here and there slight indications of French and Italian influence are discernible.

Pierre Tourguéneff contributes the only piece worthy of special notice, "*Pastour de la Steppe*," a life-size equestrian statue, is a very interesting, calm, and earnest work, with a certain amount of character. "*Fille d'Eve*," a marble statue, represents a woman lying at full length in a lazy, negligent attitude. It is a good study of the female form, and is certainly pleasing. These and other works exhibited by this artist are serious and unpretentious.

SWEDEN.

Sweden contributes two hundred and twenty-eight works to the Exhibition of Fine Arts. One hundred and fifty are oil paintings. This collection, like others furnished by nations of the north, is characterized more by rude strength than by picturesqueness or beauty. It is quite apparent from their productions that the Swedish artist has accepted the theory that has been too generally adopted, that art should have as little to do with the development of the beautiful as possible, and that those who practice it should content themselves with delineating in a mechanical and matter-of-fact way just what they see in nature and nothing more.

There are, however, among the works in this section several which show not only excellent *technique*, but go very much beyond in the way of harmonious composition and fine suggestions in color, skillfully and artistically set forth.

PAINTINGS IN OIL.

Richard Bergh, an artist of marked ability, is represented by five works. He shows to most advantage in his three portraits, which betray a decided individuality in the direction of the best methods of portraiture. Simple and unpretentious, they show the character of the subject. His "*Paysages*" is suggestive, sketchy, and true, and proves this painter to be a master of more than ordinary merit in the field of landscape.

Nils Forsberg has sent a single picture, "*La fin d'un héros; souvenir de* 1870-'71." It is large and serious in composition, and may be regarded as a fairly successful effort to commemmorate a typical scene, the death of an officer from wounds received in battle.

Auguste Hagborg is probably the best known of all the living Swedish artists, and his works are justly esteemed for their many fine qualities. He is represented at the Exhibition by eight canvases, in which his manner of treatment and style of composition are to be easily recognized. His earlier works are noted for their fine, clear, atmospheric effects and strength of drawing. A well defined purpose, combined with a just appreciation of forms, ran through them. The pictures by which he is now represented do not exhibit the fine qualities of the artist so strikingly as did those of former days.

They leave an impression of having been rather carelessly painted. The sparkling, clear grays have become almost white, and the transparent atmosphere, once so much admired, has become opaque and uncertain.

Ernest Josephson is represented by seven works. One, *"Portrait de M. R..,"* is of decided excellence, both as to quality of color and execution.

Carl Larsson shows one work, an extraordinary scheme of decoration. It is a composite of plaster and canvas, forming three panels, and intended for a private gallery at Gothenberg. The triple subject is *"La Renaissance; le* XVIII*e siecle; l'art moderne."* The principal figure is enthroned in the midst of others, which are very long, badly modeled, and faulty in drawing. Some of them are sprawled out in most ungraceful positions. The whole composition is a confused mass of lightly colored and plaster human figures, carrying no intelligible meaning. But the work must be of considerable art value, otherwise the International Jury would not have given the artist a first medal for its production.

Bruno Lilijefors is a painter of animals. Two of his four works in the Exhibition, *"Chasse aux canards"* and *"Chasse finie,"* are vigorous. The first mentioned is very truthful, freely handled, and strong in perspective. In the other the action and expression of the dogs are particularly spirited and natural.

Of the two pictures shown by Allan Österlind, *"Le baptême"* is the better. It is composed of landscape, architectural features, and children, for it is somewhat in the vein of the children's party by Knaus, although in no respect an imitation.

Mme. Hanna Pauli-Hirsch has sent three works. The *"Portrait de Mlle. V. S."* is artistically much better than the average portrait, and probably possesses the additional merit of being a truthful likeness.

Hugo Salmson is an artist of considerable invention and facility for composition. He has a weakness for French peasants, and paints them very prettily. Two of his pictures, *"Une arrestation, Picardie,"* and *"A la barriere; en Suède,"* were purchased by the French Government and form part of the Luxemburg collection.

Alfred Wahlberg, another of the well-known Swedish artists, has sent seven works, *"La lune de Septembre à l'île de Vdderón, Suède,"* and *"Soir du mois d'août à Lysekil; Suède,"* bring the scenes which they represent vividly before the spectator. The former of the two is exceptionally strong and clear in color.

Anders Zorn exhibits his vigorous painting *"Un pêcheur,"* loaned by the Luxumburg gallery, and two lifelike, broadly treated, decorative portraits.

WATER COLORS AND PASTELS.

Carl Larsson is a water colorist who uses his brush with rare facility. He contributes four works. One of these, "*Le Vin*" is in two parts. In the first is a young woman picking grapes under a trellis, and in a second an old man is drinking wine. The first is a most delicate scheme of light green and yellow. "*Jour d'Automne*," is also very pleasing in color and altogether artistic.

Robert Thegerström has two pastels. "*Le soir au village*" has a charmingly soft atmosphere, and is artistically composed.

Alf Wallender is a pastelist possessing rare power of observation and directness in expressing his ideas. He contributes five works, "*Pauvreté*," "*Intérieur d'un cabaret*," "*Deux amis*," are all story telling delineations, full of merit and interest. This artist has found out how little material it takes to make a good picture, if that little is well done.

Anders Zorn exhibits five water colors. "*Portrait de Mlle. S.*," "*Enfants*," and "*Deux filles*," are very sketchy and lightly handled.

SCULPTURE.

Pierre Hasselberg is the only Swedish sculptor whose works in the Exhibition appear to be of special interest. Two of them, "*Attrait de la vague*," and "*La petite grenouille*," are well modeled, and are serious attempts in the direction of truth.

SWITZERLAND.

Switzerland contributes one hundred and sixty-eight items to the Exhibition of Fine Arts. Among the oil paintings are to be found several that are remarkable for their robust strength and want of pictorial grace and interest. These works of art seem to partake of the ruling characteristics of the Swiss people. They are matter-of-fact in composition, rude and coarse in execution. As a rule they are not the kind that give pleasure, although they may excite curiosity.

OIL PAINTINGS.

Baud-Bovy is represented by four works. "*Bergers de l'Oberland s'excerçant au jeu de la lutte*," shows two stalwart peasants wrestling among cattle, in the high mountains. There is a certain strong, rugged fidelity to nature in the composition, but it is totally devoid of the imaginative, and would do well for the panel of a beer shop. The three other works are of the same order.

Earnest Biéler exhibits among his three canvases a large one representing a life-size group of peasant women standing in front of a church. They are painted as though they were made of blue and green porcelain, and standing upon a grass plot composed of bits of broken green glass. This artist, like the Impressionists, has made a bold dash for something new, and has not been unsuccessful. His work is possibly an artistic curiosity.

Louise Breslau contributes four oil and three water colors, and in each there is clear evidence of the true art instinct and its cultivation in the right direction. The large portrait of herself is the most original and cleverly executed work in the Swiss collection.

Eugene Bernand is probably the most successful painter of Swiss farms, bulls, cows, sheep, etc. His three representative works now exhibited belong to the three most important collections of his country. This is sufficient evidence that his pictures are greatly appreciated by his countrymen.

Jules Giradet is a painter of war scenes. Two of his four works now exhibited, "*La déroute de Cholet*," and "*Le Général de Lescure blessé, passe la Loire avec son armée en déroute*," are very spirited; the former is particularly full of action, and betrays a fair knowledge of the real movement of a war episode. In both canvases is to be perceived a serious attempt to master a difficult subject, and in each instance a fair amount of success has been attained.

Charles Giron is represented by three portraits and one of the largest canvases in the whole Exhibition. It is called "*Les deux soeurs*," and tells the old story of poverty on foot, the good sister in coarse garb, with small children in hand, while the very bad sister, dressed in costly laces and fine silks, rides in a luxurious carriage. The scene is in Paris, just in front of the Madelaine, where (in the painting) vehicles of several sorts are involved in the greatest confusion, omnibusses being driven over the steps of the church, etc. Notwithstanding the defects in drawing and perspective, the painting tells its story in an exceptionally strong manner, but without the moral, for the bad sister does not seem to suffer any considerable amount of visible punishment on this earth for her sins, and for all we know she may be sharp enough to repent in time to save herself trouble in the next. The central group (the two sisters and the carriage) is remarkably well done.

Edouard Ravel's "*Fête patronale dans le Val d'Hérens*" is a scene of peasants in a church porch among the mountains. It is rather better than such compositions usually are. The other three works by this artist are not of much interest and do not call for special notice.

Alphonse Stengelin contributes two pleasing landscapes, simple in design and general treatment, but executed with great care. "*Environs de Laaghalen, Hollande*," is especially attractive on account of its truthful, serial perspective, and fine tree forms in the middle foreground.

The other classes introduced in the Swiss section do not contain works of marked merit, nor do they present any peculiarities which need be dwelt upon.

OTHER STATES.

In addition to the countries already mentioned as exhibiting in the *Palais des Beaux Arts*, Roumania and Servia sent small collections of little artistic value.

THE INTERNATIONAL SECTION.

In the rooms set apart for the works of artists of various nationalities which arrived too late to be placed in the sections to which they belonged, a small number are of considerable merit. The works of the following artists are especially noteworthy: Arturo Michelena, of Venezuela, J. J. de Souza-Pinto, of Portugal, Thompson, of England, and Zackarie Zakarian, of Constantinople.

The Principality of Monaco, the Republic of San Marino, and Hawaii, the Argentine Republic, Bolivia, Chili, Ecuador. Guatemala, Salvador, Uruguay, and Mexico have their art exhibits combined with their industrial sections. With the exception of the pictures of Vilasco, the Mexican artist who paints the scenery of his country with ability, there is nothing that is really noteworthy in the art work contributed by these various states. The condition of art in Central and South America can not be very flourishing, if the examples set before us in the Exhibition are to be taken as a criterion. Viewed collectively, they show neither schooling nor ambition. The subjects chosen are, for the most part, trivial, and both in composition and execution they leave a good deal to be desired.

THE FRENCH WATER COLOR SOCIETY.

The French Water Color Society exhibits four hundred and sixty-three noncompetitive works, in a separate building near the *Palais des Beaux Arts*. They show a very marked falling off. During the first years after the organization of the Society of French Water Colorists, each annual Exhibition was a notable event. Only a small number of artists exhibited, but as a rule their works were of true excellence. While there are a few good examples in the present collection, it must be admitted that the large majority are in no sense representative of the best methods of water-color painting.

THE FRENCH PASTELISTS.

The French Society of Pastelists likewise occupy a separate building. It is near that containing the water colors, and includes one hundred and fifty-three works. Of the collection it may be said that it is representative of its kind, but while it leaves an impression of good artistic qualities, it does not seem to be of particular interest as a whole. The list of exhibitors contains some of the best known names connected with French art of to-day; but the work generally appears to have been done as a pastime in the leisure moments of the artists, rather than in their serious hours.

ARCHITECTURAL DRAWINGS.

In the competitive part of the Exhibition of Fine Arts are "Designs and Models in Architecture." Some three hundred exhibitors have contributed about fifteen hundred drawings. In this class France clearly takes the lead both in variety of invention and in execution. Many of the drawings, showing the restoration of the famous Greek temples of antiquity and some of the more historical buildings of the later Roman period, are notable as evidences of scholarly research and fine workmanship. Such work enables us to realize, as none other can, the glorious architectural achievements of the ancient civilizations. In the number of exhibits England comes next to France, but her work does not compare in merit with that of the French. The English exhibitors show no love for the noble Greek prototypes. Their country seems to be the hospitable home for every phase of the composite in architecture. The Dutch collection stands next to the English in importance. Several other countries show from one to sixteen numbers, presenting nothing more remarkable than fair office work.

GENERAL REMARKS.

The foregoing remarks close this report so far as it relates to the exhibition of contemporary art. The writer has sought to draw attention to the better known artists, and those of acknowledged superiority, representing every country, and especially to indicate the work of those who appear to him to be on the right path. If his descriptive or critical remarks have any practical value, it must be in so far as they may assist the reader to form some impression of the contemporary art movements throughout the world. The very large number of works exhibited has rendered the task of mentioning even the names of all deserving artists one of great difficulty, which for many selfevident reasons the writer did not attempt to complete.

THE RETROSPECTIVE EXHIBITION OF FRENCH ART.

A very attractive, instructive, and possibly in several respects, the most important portion of the Fine Arts section of the Exhibition, was the *"Exposition Centennale de l'Art Français* (1789–1889)." This collection was composed of oil paintings, 652; drawings and water colors, 558; miniatures and fans, 76; sculptures, 140; medals, 129; architectural drawings, 376; engravings and lithographs, 465; total, 2,396.

These several classes forming the retrospective collection, were arranged under and in the immediate vicinity of the " *Dome* "of the *"Palais des Beaux Arts."* The sculpture on the ground floor, and the exhibits forming the other classes in the galleries of the second floor under the dome, and extending into and occupying several large galleries adjoining.

THE DOME.

The dome which crowns the center of the Palace of Fine Arts is one of the most beautiful structures of its kind in existence. Artistically poised upon slender and graceful supports, jauntily lifted into the air, seemingly without effort, lighted from four sides by four long windows located immediately under the spring of the dome, as well as from the top, and delicately and artistically decorated in imitation of light tile work, it is like a dream of architectural abstraction, novel in design and construction, and fascinating in all the details of its adornment. It became at once a leading attraction and a distinctive feature of the Exhibition, and when regarded in connection with the historic and beautiful objects it partially covered, its powers to fascinate the sense of the beautiful has seldom been rivaled. Its decoration is so effectually illusive that the unsympathetic surface of the iron and glass with which it was constructed are completely subordinated to an exceptional triumph of art over the most belligerently in artistic combination of building materials known. It may be said of the whole group popularly known as the "Main Buildings" of the Exhibition, and constructed of those materials, that it is the only iron and glass structure on a large scale, which, from an aesthetic and architectural standpoint, ought to be permitted to exist.

While the retrospective collection was not as to important names quite complete, it was comprehensively illustrative of the preceding century of French art, the merits and demerits of the century's work were fully set forth, and never before was there such a compact opportunity for studying the varying phases of national characteristics and fashions in all branches of a national art.

OIL PAINTINGS—DAVID—MANET.

The oil paintings represented one hundred and thirteen deceased, and seventy-six living artists. The two extremes of the century were seen in the works of David and Manet. The carefully constructed compositions of the former prove that he knew the value of Greek forms, and that he was imbued with the poetic spirit which animated the great masters who gave the world its finest examples of classic art. The latter was the master of a very free hand, and a believer in the largest liberty, who acknowledged neither the restraints of any known *technique* as taught, nor the obligations imposed by nature, and his works prove that he was governed by an abiding faith in methods that had, at least, the virtue of being his own. To the large majority of individuals however, of average culture and understanding, the greater part of his work is incomprehensible, while to others a hidden purpose of great artistic import is discovered in the least important of his productions. It may be said of his reputation that it is based upon and measured by the strength of his originality and boldness as an irreverent innovator, rather than upon the real art value of his work. To this assertion there are exceptions. As in the history of all known exceptionals, so it is with this one. Sometimes from out the depths of their mysterious imaginations and methods there comes a simple manifestation of straightforward individualism that all can understand. In this instance one of the exceptions exhibited was a painting entitled "*Le Bon Bock*,"—Catalogue number, 489. It is a portrait of a happy specimen of humanity who knew the value of beer and tobacco. This presentation is in a vein quite the artist's own, but without affectation or exaggeration, and is so true and suggestive of a type that it would lose nothing of its merit by being hung in company with the characteristic work of Hals and other great Dutch artists who painted the beer drinkers and smokers of their times.

DAVID.

David was born in 1748, studied under Vien, the director for many years of the French Academy at Rome, and was one of the best among the French painters of that period of mannerisms. In 1772 he gained the second prize at the Royal Academy; in 1775 the grand prize, and with it a pension which enabled him to go with his master to Rome, where he devoted himself to the study of the antique and historical painting. In 1780 he returned to Paris and three years after was appointed painter to the king. In 1784 he returned to Rome and in that year painted for Louis XVI the "Oath of the Horatii," and finished his "Belisarius;" in 1787 he executed the "Death of Socrates," and in 1788 his "Paris and Helen." In 1789 we find him again in Paris, an ardent believer in the new order of things, and the chief art promoter of the revolutionary fêtes and monuments. The works completed previous to the revolution are regarded as the greatest of his first or purely classic period, and their execution stand for an important landmark in the history of modern French art.

It will thus be seen that his commanding position had been assured before the breaking out of the great movement which was to annihilate the power of a royal family, and build anew an old nation. It was from this last-named period to 1889, inclusive, that the late retrospective exhibition was intended to cover, or in other words, the one hundred years of a national life under the new order.

The talent of David as displayed in his works, and the debt that modern art owes to his influence in the right direction, are the excuses for the frequent reference to him in this communication.

LATER FRENCH PAINTERS.

Between the extremes of the classic style of David and the icon-
oclastic deviations of Manet, there was a wide field which has been
covered with infinite skill by artists of marked individuality, masters of *technique* and the art of picturesque composition. But in
this report it is only possible to mention the names of the more conspicuous among them, who, since the culminating point in the career
of the founder, have accomplished so much for the present ascend-
ancy of French art.   There is no pretense that the list is complete, as it
contains only the names and dates of birth of prominent artists,
whose reputations for good work have been recognized and fully
established in the later history of art.   Among the names of those
deceased are to be found :

Drolling	1732	Isabey	1804
Lebrun, Mme	1755	Diaz	1808
Vernet	1758	Troyon	1810
Watteau	1758	Rousseau, T	1812
Prudéhon	1760	Millet	1814
Girodet	1767	Muller	1815
Gerard	1770	Couture	1815
Gros	1771	Daubigny, C. F.	1817
Guerin	1774	Courbet	1819
Ingres	1780	Fromentin	1820
Coignet	1791	Cabanel	1824
Géricault	1791	Brascassat	1824
Corot	1796	Baudry	1828
Delaroche	1797	de Neuville	1835
Delacroix	1798	Regnault	1843
Déchamps	1803	Bastien Lepage	1848
Dupré	....		

Among living artists whose works have attained a high standard
of excellence, which is generally admitted by writers and connois-
seurs, may be mentioned the names of Bonheur, Bonnat, Bouguereau, Breton, Carolus-Duran, Cazin, Chaplin, Collin, F. Cormon,
Dagnan-Bouveret, Detaille, Duez, Français, Gerome, Gervex, Harpignies, Herbert, Henner, Humbert, Laurens, Lefebvre, Lhermitte
Luminais, Maignan, Meissonier, Morot, Pelouse, Pointelin, Puvis
de Chavannes, Roll, Tattegrain, Weber, Ziem, and Zuber. Many
more names might with propriety be added to each class, but a sufficient number has been cited to give the reader some idea of the masters amongst the French painters who have made notable reputations during the preceding century.

WATER COLORS AND DRAWINGS.

The water colors and drawings were especially interesting and possibly more distinctively characteristic as to nationality, than any
other portion of the retrospective display.   This suggestion is par-

ticularly applicable to the works of the illustrators and caricaturists of the past, which in most instances possess a pure national flavor coupled with the individuality of the artists. Their powers of exaggeration sometimes falling only a little short of the grotesque, and often going beyond, enabled them to send their arrows of satire through the thin coverings of folly, vice, and crime in a manner peculiar to themselves and beyond the power of imitation by others. The old water colors, as to distinctive characteristics, were quite by themselves and unlike any similar work by the artists of to-day, and were chiefly interesting from an antiquarian standpoint, as illustrating the styles in vogue a half a century and more ago. The better known artists represented by works in this class were Barye, Baudry, Boilly, Coignet, Courbet, Couture, Daumier, David, Decamps, Delacroix, Dutertre, Fragonard, Garvarni, Gérard, Géricault, Grandville, Ingres, Isabey, Johannot, Millet, de Neuville, Prudhon, Regnault, A. Vernet, Watteau, and others quite as well known.

SCULPTURE.

The collection of exhibits in the retrospective representing French sculptors, although not extensive, was of marked interest and almost as national in its leading features as either of the other classes. Much of the work was strongly individual, even the purely academic examples of the pronounced formalists was positively national in its treatment and expression, so much so that it could never be mistaken for other than French work.

HOUDON.

Standing out by itself and quite alone in the strength of its modest simplicity, was the work of Houdon. His three busts, Franklin, Lafayette, and Napoleon, fully attested the rare faculty of this artist for delineating the character of his subjects. In the presence of these works, while contemplating their simple lines and careful construction, we feel perfectly sure of their exceptional value as truthful portraits. Upon the invitation of Franklin, this artist visited America and executed, from life, a full length statue of Washington, which is now in the capitol building of Virginia at Richmond.

MEDALS.

The number of medals exhibited was insignificant, and did not represent the last one hundred years of French effort in the direction of representative medallic work. Many of the greatest names were missing from the catalogue, and of those present only a small number are recognized as masters. The leading feature in this class was the proof portraits, which were of exceptional merit as to design and execution. These could have been supplemented from out the great

resources of the "Hotel des Monnaies," and a collection brought together worthy of the occasion and the nation that stands at the head
in this particular field.

ARCHITECTURE.

The architectural drawings by fifty-one deceased and twenty-six
living architects covered a period from the time of Brougniart, Cas-
sas, Fontaine, Baltard, and Percier to the present. Although not as
extensive as the collection of architectural drawings in the competitive part of the group, it was more interesting, and for the same
reason which applied to the other classes of the "Centennale." It
gave those interested in modern French, or we might almost say
national, architecture an opportunity to study past fashions and the
capacity of architects for purely artistic work. It enabled them to
observe intelligently the growth and gradual crystallization into present styles and forms of the various kinds of prevailing French
architecture.

Many of these drawings in black and white and in water colors
displayed a rare knowledge of purely technical drawing, and, in several instances, the poetic instinct for the beautiful. But it is quite
certain that very few, if any, of the works in the old collection
could, as to artistic excellence in execution, be compared with the
better of those in the competitive collection by living architects.

ENGRAVING AND LITHOGRAPHY.

Under the title of Engraving and Lithography there was an exceptional display of old and new impressions. Very much of the meritorious work was by artists now living, and the better of all was the
etchings which formed a conspicuous part of this class. The specimens displayed proved conclusively that several of the great painters were experts in the use of the etching needle and graver. It would
have been difficult to have selected a single number from their exhibits which would not stand the test of sound, critical examination.
Where there was so much that was good, it would be futile to
attempt even to point out the best from among the numbers conspicuous for excellence. In this list of contributions by living artists,
remarkable for their fine qualities, were the works of Bonnat,
Flameng, Achille and Jules Jacquet, and Meissonier, which in several
instances were veritable monuments of their kind.

Among the deceased artists whose work worthily represented their
reputation were to be found the names of Bonvin, Corot, Daubigny,
Decamps, Delacroix, Jacquemart, Manet, Proudhon, and T. Rousseau. Others not so well known, but of equal merit, were fittingly
represented.

After the etchers came a long list of engravers and lithographers.
A considerable portion of this work was devoted to designs by past

caricaturists and illustrators; and from an art standpoint much of it was very poor "stuff" but not uninteresting. The old colored lithographs carried the memory back to the beginning of the flash and florid in the advertising of quackeries; and the work of the illustrators recalled to our minds the early editions of Sue, Dumas, Balzac, and a host of other popular French authors of forty and fifty years ago; while the comic genius of the caricaturists, united with a rare combination of natural instinct for satire, brought graphically to the mind of the spectator the follies and vices of French social life and much of the political intrigue which has taken place in France since the days of the revolution.

REMARKS AT END OF TECHNICAL REPORT.

The preceding paragraph brings to a close the portion of this report specially devoted to the art collections known in official language as " *Groupe I*," displayed by themselves in the " *Palais des Beaux Arts.*" The notes upon which its descriptive and critical remarks are founded were taken at odd times while the Exhibition was in progress and when the writer was actively engaged in other official duties that occupied the better part of his time, and are necessarily incomplete.

It now goes to its official destination without apology for its short-comings or excuse for the, in many instances, strong phraseology employed to express decided opinions. There is no pretense that many of the unpopular sentiments expressed or judgments pronounced as to the merits of the works of certain artists are correct. For them the claim of infallibility is not made, but they have at least the single virtue of expressing the unqualified convictions of one who has traveled much, seen very much of the world's better art, and has tried to profit by his valuable opportunities. It is, however, a matter of regret to the writer that he could not bring to the performance of his duties, critical and literary, the technical knowledge possessed by those who practice the arts, coupled with the style and literary ability of the accomplished writer.

Through the whole of this report two leading considerations have been kept steadily in view—the exaltation of simplicity and truth and the unqualified condemnation of the meretricious. In our country the absence of the two former qualities and the ever-present abundance of the latter constitute sins of omission and commission of great magnitude, which can only be corrected by the very slow process of national education; and if it shall turn out that only a small number of individuals after reading this communication shall start out to find for themselves the great truths which are manifestly applicable to the arts, the writer will feel that his labors were not without useful results.

METHOD OF SELECTING THE ART EXHIBITS.

At the time of accepting the appointment as the official head of Group I, I was aware of the difficulties I would have to encounter and had some little conception of the obstacles that would present themselves as stumbling-blocks in the road to success, and from the first had determined, as far as possible, to sink my individuality in favor of those (the artists) most interested, and after considerable deliberation with others, fixed upon the plan of selecting a jury from among the members of the National Academy of Design and the Society of American Artists, and the seventeen who were selected for this duty were taken from names recommended by the officers of these organizations. Early in the spring of 1889, and before action had been had in New York, the American artists living in and near Paris held a mass meeting and appointed from among themselves a jury of seventeen to make selections from among the works of American artists living abroad, and both in New York and Paris these bodies were intrusted with the power of selection and rejection. It may be mentioned that the exhibits accepted in each city were about one in three. The work of choosing on both sides of the ocean was performed in good faith, without fear or favor, and all errors were on the side of mercy. For it is a fact that at least fifty oil paintings were admitted which were of no advantage to our art section, and were calculated to belittle the value of the better work and to mar the *tout ensemble* of the whole.

INDEPENDENT HEAD FOR ART DEPARTMENT.

In the great exhibitions held abroad it had been, I believe, customary to make the Fine Arts a separate department, kept distinct from the other sections and under the direction of an independent head. M. Antonin Proust was the late special art commissioner appointed by the French authorities, who had sole charge of Group I, and I am certain that the wonderful success achieved in that group was largely due to the fact of the untrammeled and independent action of that official, and I know that several art sections of other nations were under the control of persons independent of any official connected with other departments, and I am perfectly certain that it would always be for the better interests at least of the arts when brought together for exhibition, that their supervision should be in the hands of an entirely independent official, and I unhesitatingly close this report with a recommendation to that effect.

NEW YORK, *March* 4, 1890.

A classified table showing the total number of art exhibits from all countries and comprised in Group I.

Countries.	Class I.— Oil paintings.	Class II.— Different kinds of paintings and drawings (water colors, pastels, black and white).	Class III.— Sculpture and engraving on medals.	Class IV.— Drawings and models in architecture.	Class V.— Engravings and lithography.	Total number of exhibits of each country.
France....	1,418	213	561	138	444	2,774
Algeria	85	10	9	11	....	65
Colonies	1	2	4	....	....	7
Germany	64	24	4	....	....	92
Austria-Hungary	124	15	18	.. ..	2	159
Belgium	252	34	53	38	71	448
Denmark	190	9	17	7	3	226
Spain	116	40	8	1	15	180
United States	336	117	16	1	102	572
Finland	56	2	17	....	2	77
Great Britain	172	176	39	93	72	552
Greece	46	10	25	6	4	91
Italy	188	33	98	5	3	327
Norway ...	125	6	10	.. ..	2	143
Netherlands	174	43	2	31	38	288
Roumania	135	4	16	4	....	50
Russia .	146	21	32	....	3	205
Servia	20	....	6	....	....	26
Sweden	150	42	30	2	4	228
Switzerland.....	92	21	19	16	20	168
International	49	8	5	....	....	62
Luxembourg.................	....	....	3	....	....	3
Principality of Monaco	6	1	4	1	....	12
Republic of St. Marin	....	1	1	1	....	3
Hawaii......................	1	....	....	....	1	2
Argentine Republic...........	....	....	3	1	3	7
Bolivia.......................	4	2	.. ..	2	....	8
Chili	25	....	7	....	....	32
Ecuador	....	1	3	....	....	2
Guatemala	17	2	3	....	2	24
Salvador.....................	19	1	2	4	....	26
Uruguay.....................	11	3	.. ..	....	....	14
Mexico......................	25	....	3	....	....	28
	3,897	844	1,018	362	701	6,912
France, Centennial Retrospective....................	652	634	269	376	465	2,396
Water colors.................	....	463	....	....	....	463
Pastels......................	....	153	....	....	....	153
Designs. various, from state manufactories and provincial schools, estimated....	....	....	....	....	....	2,000
Total..............	4,549	2,094	1,287	738	1,256	11,034

JURIES.

CLASSES I AND II.

OIL PAINTINGS, DIFFERENT KINDS OF PAINTINGS AND DRAWINGS.

OFFICERS.

Meissonier, J. L. Ernest, *President*, France.
Artz, D. A. Constant, *Vice President*, Netherlands.
Lafenestre, Georges, *Rapporteur*, France.
Dannat, William T., *Secretary*, United States.

MEMBERS.

Bonnat, Léon.............. ...France.
Bouguereau, A. William..........do...
Breton, A. Jules.................do...
Carolus-Duran, E. A..............do...
Cazin, J. Charles........ ....do...
Duez, Ernest A....................do...
Fantin-Latour, Henry J. T........do...
Fourcaud, Louis de...............do...
Français, F. Louis...............do...
Gérôme, Jean Léon. ....do...
Gervex, Henri....................do...
Henner, Jean Jacques............do...
Laurens, Jean Paul...............do...
Mantz, Paul........ ....do...
Puvis de Chavannes, Pierre.......do ..
Roll, Alfred P.... ....do...
Vollon, Antoine.................do...
Jettel, Eugène de......Austria-Hungary.

Portaels, Jean ....Belgium.
Robie, Jean.....................do...
Verlat, Charles..................do...
Tuxen, L................... Denmark.
Mélida, Enrique................Spain.
Hawkins, General R. C...United States.
Pearce, Charles S.................do...
Armitage, Edward......Great Britain.
Davis, H. W. B..................do...
Ouless, W. W.....................do...
Besnard, Albert .. ..Greece.
Pittara, Charles..................Italy.
Becker, A. de............... Finland.
Skredsvig, Christian..........Norway.
Willy-Martens ....Netherlands.
Pranishnikoff, Ivan .. ..Russia.
Salmson, Hugo...............Sweden.
Meuron, A. de............Switzerland.

International section.

Heilbuth, Ferdinand.... .... | Kuehl, Gotthardt....... ....

SUPPLEMENTARY JURY.

Michel, André.................France.
Busson, Charles...................do...
Galland, O ....do...
Gosselin, Charles ....do...
Hamel, Maurice...................do...
Harpignies, Henri...............do...
Lerolle, Henri...................do...
Deschamps, Charles W...Great Britain.

Thoren, Otto de..... Austria-Hungary.
Robert, Alexandre...........Belgium.
Frolich, Lorenz.............Denmark.
Beruete, A. de... ....Spain.
Bartlett, Paul W........United States.
Rossi, Luigi.....................Italy.
Thaulow, Fritz................Norway.
Hagborg, Auguste............Sweden.

International Section.

Roger-Ballu.

CLASS III.

SCULPTURE AND ENGRAVINGS ON MEDALS.

OFFICERS.

Guillaume, Cl. J. B. Eugéne, *President*, France.
Groot, Guillaume de, *Vice President*, Belgium,
Kaempfen, Albert, *Rapporteur*, France.
Gille, P. H., France, *Secretary*, France.

MEMBERS.

Cavelier, Pierre Jules...........France.	Saglio, Edmond.................France.
Chaplain, Jules Clément.........do...	Beer, Frederick de ...Austria-Hungary.
Chapu, Henri M. A...............do...	Thornycroft, Hamo.......Great Britain.
Dubois, Paul....................do...	Rossano, J.......................Italy.
Falguière, Alexandre............do...	Romanelli, R................ ....do...
Frémiet, Emmanuel...... ......do...	Hasselberg, Pierre............Sweden.
Lefeuvre, Albert................do...	Rohmann, Robert............Russia.
Rodin, Auguste.................do...	Bisbing, Henry S.........United States.

SUPPLEMENTARY JURY.

Courajod, Louis...............France. | Marquiset, L. H...............France.

CLASS IV.

DRAWINGS AND MODELS IN ARCHITECTURE.

OFFICERS.

Bailly, Antoine Nicholas, *President*, France.
Waterhouse, J. W., *Vice President*, Great Britain.
Baudot, de, *Rapporteur*, France.
Pascal, J. Louis, *Secretary*, France.

MEMBERS.

André, Jules..................France.	Lisch, Juste....................France.
Boeswillwald, Emile.............do...	Vaudremer, Joseph A. E.........do ..
Garnier, J. L. Charles..........do...	White, W. P.............Great Britain.

SUPPLEMENTARY JURY.

Magne, Lucien............ .....France.	Pauli, A.....................Belgium.
Moyaux, Const..................do...	

CLASS V.

ENGRAVINGS AND LITHOGRAPHY.

OFFICERS.

·Delaborde, le Vicomte, *President*, France.
Biot, Gustave, *Vice President*, Belgium.
Bracquemond, Felix, *Rapporteur*, France.
Stewart, Julius L., *Secretary*, United States.

MEMBERS.

Blanchard, Emile, O............France.	Waltner, Charles A.............France.
Flameng, Léopold...............do...	

SUPPLEMENTARY JURY.

Béraldi, M, France.

Table alphabetically arranged, giving the number of awards alloted to the different countries at the Paris Exhibition, 1889.

Countries	Medals of honor.					First-class medals (gold).					Second-class medals (silver).					Third-class medals (bronze).					Honorable mentions.					Total.
	I	II	III	IV	V	I	II	III	IV	V	I	II	III	IV	V	I	II	III	IV	V	I	II	III	IV	V	
Algeria											3						3		1				1			3
Austria-Hungary	1					3					9					10		1			12		2			33
Argentine Republic																										
Bolivia																										
Belgium	3		4	1		6		3	1	1	9		4	2	2	25	1	5			8	1	2	2	3	84
Brazil								1	1		1			2		1					2					7
Chili	1			1		3	1	1			6		1			10					21		1			51
Denmark											5		1			6		3			4		3			
Ecuador																										
Finland																										
France	13		9	10	5	59	4	43	24	14	91	7	49	23	13	186	39	81	36	17	130	11	38	17	13	911
Germany	2		2	2	1	1			2	2	3	2	1	5	2	9	1	5	5	1	7	1	1			29
Great Britain	2				1	10	7				12	12	1	2		26	13	2			11	2	2			129
Greece											1		1			6		1					2			14
Guatemala											1					6										1
Hawaiian Islands																										
Italy			3			6	2	3			6	3	4			24		8	1		21	4		3		115
International section						2					3					6		1	1							13
Luxembourg						2										2		1						1		1
Mexico			3					1					1					1	1							9
Norway	1					2	1	1			1	3		1		2	1	1			1	1	1	1		36
Netherlands	1										8					7				2	14		1			61
Principality of Monaco											11					16					15					2
Republic of St. Marin						2					6					7		1								1
Russia	1		1			4	1			1	6	2	2	1		15	1	2	2		8		1			46
Roumania			1				1				2					1		1			6		3			16

																									Total
Spain	1			3	2				8	1	1	1	1	14	3	2		11		3					51
Servia									1					1				1							5
Sweden	1			2	1		1		6	1	1	1		9		2		12	1	2		3			44
Switzerland				3	2		2		3		1			15	3	2		12		2		3			48
Salvador																									
United States	2		1	4	2		1		14	6			2	38	2	1	2	24	2	4		4		3	110
Uruguay														1				2							3
Total	31	21	13	7	110	21	55	28	19	200	39	66	39	21	431	50	120	47	24	324	32	101	26	21	1,846

RECAPITULATION.

Numbers of medals of honor including the five classes........................ 72
Number of first-class medals (gold), including the five classes.............. 233
Number of second-class medals (silver), including the five classes 365
Number of third-class medals (bronze), including the five classes 672
Number of honorable mentions, including the five classes 504

[Journal des Débats, September 22, 1889.]

The painters of the United States travel a great deal; they are very well informed as to what happens abroad, and they don't disdain on occasion to profit by their knowledge. We find in their Exhibition, very interesting by the way, more than one reminder of Jules Dupré, Théodore Rousseau, Cazin, Millet, Jules Breton, and of Whistler—who is, by the way, American by birth and English by adoption—of Puvis de Chavannes, of the Japanese artists, of Mr. Gérôme, and even of Mr. Bouguereau, whose conceptions are repeated in Miss Elizabeth Gardner. There is, however, one trait which distinguishes them; it is a certain incisive and cold manner, phlegmatic and, as it were, indifferent. What they do undoubtedly interests them, since they do it; what they paint pleases them; but they seem to bring to it, for the most part, a rare power of objectivity. *Nil admirari* is their motto; don't try to astonish them, don't try either to surprise them, *flagrante delicto*, in a fit of enthusiasm; they don't yield to it, and they will detect the attempt.

Mr. J. Gari Melchers, a pupil of Messrs. Lefèbvre and Boulanger, has chosen his residence in the Frisian cantons of Holland. The marked types of the peasants, their dress, their manners interest him. It is impossible to put more precision, penetration, strength, and frigidity, I do not say impersonality, into a *procès-verbal*, than he has put into his remarkable studies, "The Pilots," "The Sermon," and "Communion." We have known these pictures already from having seen them in former Salons; no one will regret seeing them again.

Mr. William Dannat, who calls himself a pupil of Munkacsy on the catalogue, made his début in the atelier of Carolus Duran; he seems to-day to incline towards Whistler. "A Quartette" and "A Sacristy in Aragon" are in his first manner, less self-contained, less subtle; but we admire in them at once a rare delicacy of eye, and his individuality is clearly written. The profile of the blonde in "A Study in Red," portrait of a woman in white, tone upon tone, reveals aspirations more and more refined, a great sureness of hand, and the most delicious talent.

The "View at Venice," of Mr. Ralph Curtis, all in tender rose, fine violet, light amber, and subtle lilac colors; "Evening by the Lake," of W. S. Allen, pupil of Messrs. Bouguereau, J. Lefèbvre, and Claude Monot; "A City Park," "Stoneyard," and "A Bit of Long Island," of Mr. William Chase (who exhibits also some very good portraits), and a "Peace," all in white on a charming silver-blue ground, are of exquisite expression.

One is much suprised to find alongside of these clear, luminous, and distinctly modern pictures landscapes which appear to have been painted thirty or forty years ago, like those of Messrs. Gifford, Minor, Henry, etc., inspired no doubt by the Jules Duprés and Diazs imported into America.

There is much charm, a charm a little sad, in "A Winter Eve," "The Valley (evening)," and "Evening after the Storm," of Mr. Charles Davis, as also in "The Shepherdess," "Evening," and "Melancholy," of Mr. Charles Sprague Pearce (a pupil of Bonnat). "The Wave," of Mr. Alexander Harrison (a pupil of Gérôme and of Bastien Lepage), would be a pure *chef-d'œuvre* if the foreground were not a little hard. It is impossible to paint with a more delicate sentiment and a finer tone the tremulous light which on a clear morning shimmers with a tender and changing rose the milky-green of the sleeping sea.

Mr. John Sargent was born at Florence of American parents; he is a pupil of Mr. Carolus Duran, and, like Whistler, is established in London, where his talent for portrait painting is highly appreciated. He is a nervous painter, and consequently unequal. We had already seen the charming portrait of children which he exhibits, but that of "Mrs. W." in white satin, pearl necklace, a fan in her hand, standing on a ground of amber grey and pale gold, is of a fine and spirited elegance.

What is a little wanting in this American Exhibition is native painting on native subjects. We doubtless find it here and there in Messrs. Ulrich, Inness, Whittredge, and Simmons, for example, but it is not marked. Messrs. Mosler, Knight, Vail, Delachaux, Stewart, Bridgman, Weeks, Mac-Ewen, Boggs, Bisbing, Butler, Walker, Gay, Thayer, and Hitchcock (pupils of Messrs. Boulanger, Lefèbvre, Bouguereau, Bonnat, Gervex, Roll, Dagnan-Bouveret, Hébert, J. P. Laurens, Gérôme, Colin, etc.) go to Holland, to Brittany, to Normandy, to Touraine, to the banks of the Oise, or even remain in Paris. They are, however, for the most part, good recruits for the young American school and everything tells us that we must take it more and more into serious consideration.

ANDRÉ MICHEL.